LIFE-WORK

Life-Work

MEANINGFUL EMPLOYMENT
IN AN AGE OF LIMITS

WILLIAM A. CHARLAND, JR.

CONTINUUM

NEW YORK

1986
The Continuum Publishing Company
370 Lexington Avenue, New York, N.Y. 10017

Printed in the United States of America

Designed by Tom Mellers

Library of Congress Cataloging-in-Publication Data

Charland, William A., 1937–
Life-work.

Bibliography: p.
1. Vocational guidance. 2. Work. 3. Conduct of life.
I. Title.
HF5381.C578 1986   331.7′02   86-16837
ISBN 0-8264-0371-9

CONTENTS

PREFACE

A famous playwright was asked why he wrote plays. "Good question!" he said. "I found myself raising it last night at my neighborhood bordello: 'How did you get into this line of work?' I asked my companion. Her response describes my own career. 'At first,' she said, 'I did it because I enjoyed it. Then I did it to please people. And now I'm in it for the money!'"

This is a book about work in relation to the rest of our lives. Part of it is pragmatic, summarizing some of the techniques I have found effective in my work as a career counselor and adult educator throughout the past fifteen years. During the course of that time, I have worked with more than a thousand adults from a broad range of backgrounds. A number of them, from whom I have learned a great deal, appear in case material throughout the book.

Other sections elaborate a view of employment that is intended to reach deeper and range farther than the typical literature on seeking work. I believe that we are living in a time when the very nature and meaning of work are changing radically. Presently, about one-third of American workers are leaving their jobs every year. Some are seeking new opportunities at a perplexing time when an estimated one-third of work roles that will be important in the near future do not yet exist. Others are frustrated as they compete for a shrinking pool of jobs that are familiar. In all, it is a time for thoughtful people to reconsider the nature and place of work in their lives, while taking steps to move forward. That's what this book is intended to help the reader accomplish.

My approach to seeking work is based on an understanding of "employment" in its original sense of involvement (from Latin, *implicare*). Working is a way of being in the world, and the essence of employment is to find a place where someone wants what we can do. John Gardner's character, Arnold the cook, says it best in *The Art of Living*:

> The thing a person's gotta have—a human being—is some kind of center to his life, some one thing he's good at that other people need from him, like, for instance shoemaking. I mean something ordinary but at the same time holy, if you know what I mean.

Finding that kind of employment is a quest we all share. I invite you now to explore it.

Acknowledgments

This book owes much to many quiet collaborators: hundreds of clients and students who have chosen to include me as a partner in their growth; Joann Albright and Tom Goodale, colleagues at the University of Denver; and, most of all, Phoebe Lawrence—my wife, text editor, and constantly supportive friend.

Editorial Method

Citations of source material appear parenthetically throughout the book, usually by author's last name and page number. These refer to the work listed under the author's name in the Bibliography. If more than one by the author is listed, title—or key word in the title—also is provided.

PART I

A New Vision of Work

CHAPTER 1

THE MIRAGE
OF PERFECT WORK

"Unhappy at work? Between jobs? Looking for a career with a future? Let us teach you the techniques of successful job hunting!" In Sunday newspapers, radio, all the media, the ads appear. A cacaphony of promises, trafficking in hope, addressing the millions of Americans who are struggling in their working lives. Whether unemployed, underemployed, or misemployed, these frustrated workers present an interested audience for those who would offer solutions to our contemporary problems of employment.

Too often, the answers and resources represented by the ads are inadequate to address the real human needs related to work in our time. Sometimes the promises are deceitful; many of the high-priced career counseling franchises have become objects of litigation and regulation, as they have promised benefits they never hoped to deliver. (For a list of some recent articles on the career counseling industry and a review of other kinds of agencies, see the appendix.)

More often, the career resources available to us are simply

ill-conceived. They offer inadequate methods of treating symptoms whose root causes are not really understood—partly because the fundamental difficulties in working today result from profound changes in economic conditions and values far beneath the surface of events.

Understanding the societal side of employment is fundamental, I believe, to seeking work effectively as individuals. For without some broad, realistic perspective of the changing nature and meaning of work, we will suffer from shortsightedness—experiencing limitations we encounter as somehow our fault, or spoiling our relationships with others as we scramble to compete for a diminishing number of desirable jobs.

The best way to begin looking for work is to stop for a moment and survey our surroundings, exploring the changing meaning of employment in our society. Then we will be in a position to move forward in a direction that has significance for us. And along the way we may discover some bedrock principles and strategies that can help us all find our way through a most confusing time.

THE CHANGING MEANING OF WORK

Why do we work? In *Careers Tomorrow*, futurist Willis Harmon observes that work fulfills three essential human needs: to produce necessary goods and services, to distribute income, and to provide people with meaningful roles in society (pp. 103–104). I find that a good analysis, and would add only one other need: to find some lasting significance in what we do.

Psalm 90:17 expresses that need as a prayer based upon the Biblical Hebrew noun for "hand" (connoting strength) and two verbs that we translate "to make or do" and "to make firm, stable, steadfast" (as, for example, building a house in the desert on pillars). So, "establish Thou the work of our hands upon us, yea, the work of our hands establish Thou it!" Or, "May our strength be invested in something steadfast. May the substance of what we do endure!" That's a fundamental need as well.

Were those all of our reasons for working, I believe that we could negotiate our passage through these times more easily than we do. But our human complexity is such that our needs never fully account for our behavior. Our needs are compounded by wants that always exceed whatever we require. When it comes to work, some of us may have exceptional expectations: for example, that work have meaning. And the quest for meaning can go to extremes. So, Peter Gillingham writes in his contribution to *Good Work* by the late E. F. Schumacher:

> Work is good when it engages what Huston Smith and others have called "the vertical dimension" of life, the deepest and highest values and motivations that underlie the universe and all human life and activity. To see work as a day-to-day expression of value makes it far more than economic significance. Then it is *no less than the place where our temporal and spiritual dimensions converge.* (p. 215, emphasis added)

That's asking quite a lot of work!

Others of us may want to feel important through our work, and have fun. V. S. Naipaul's character, Harry deTunja, a Caribbean businessman, shares this fanciful vision of "good work."

> Nothing too big. No fun in running something that get too big and you can't feel it. I get to the office before anybody else. I find it cool and quiet and clean. I love being in a clean office first thing in the morning. Nobody around you, nobody talking, your desk empty. That's when I do my thinking, in that first half hour. All kinds of fantastic ideas come to me. I see how I have to play this and play that, and I feel in control. Then the guys start coming in, the letters come up, and work starts. In the middle of the morning the guys come in with some problem that is driving them frantic. Well, I listen to them and I go through the papers and I straightaway see how you have to play the thing. I say so-so-so-so. And the guys fall back in amazement. And they know why I am the boss. Well, lunchtime. . . . In the afternoon I dictate half a dozen magnificent

letters. I've been turning them over in my head all day, and at three o'clock I call the girl in and I'm ready to go. And that's it. Eight or nine problems. All settled, and I feel I can look forward to developments. I'm planning years ahead, you know. At four o'clock I'm feeling damn good. And everything I do now is like a reward.   (Naipaul, *Guerrillas*, p. 167ff.)

Of course, there is nothing wrong with seeking meaning, enjoyment, or a sense of personal importance in our work. But, as the passages I've cited suggest, human wants are boundless. There is an infinite, limitless quality to what we can wish for. Our wants can give rise to expectations that, realistically, may be difficult to satisfy.

Wants that are unexamined in a culture are very much like mirages—images of distant objects that are misperceived as close at hand. A mirage is different from a hallucination. Even in their most complex and confusing form—the fata morgana such as mountain ranges in the sky—mirages do reflect elements of reality. But the images of mirages are distorted, and they call attention to distant phenomena that can divert us from important matters close at hand.

Many Americans today live encumbered by a mirage of "perfect work." The wants represented in this mirage—for high levels of meaning, enjoyment, and feelings of personal importance—are not without basis in reality. Under earlier conditions of an expanding economy, as I shall describe, many people found this kind of employment. Even today, some who live by the vision of perfect work live very well.

But many others of us are discovering that the mirage of perfect work is groundless. We live at a time when the nature and meaning of work are changing. Most of us need to take a closer look at work, distinguishing what we have been taught to want from realistic approaches to employment in a new age of limits. The best way to see our situation clearly is to look at the mirage of perfect work from the vantage point of recent history.

A CLOSE LOOK AT ACHIEVEMENT

The expectation that personal fulfillment can be achieved through work has a very short history. Human beings have always worked. Jesus was a carpenter; Paul made tents. Presumably, both did a good job. But for all their concern with discovering meaning in life and a deep sense of personal identity, neither Jesus nor Paul appears to have found any particular significance in what he did for a living. Work was simply a part of life. Indeed, throughout the Middle Ages right up through the time of Martin Luther, one searches in vain to find anything especially good said about earning a living. Luther's understanding of the term "calling," for example, connoted simply the station of life in which a person found himself. One's position was to be accepted and tolerated, if not celebrated. And any attempt to transcend that place in life—as, for example, seeking spiritual virtuosity in a monastery—was discouraged. Work, for Jesus, Paul, and Luther, was simply a given—an inevitable part of life.

The changing meaning of work appears, in the history of Christian thought, with John Calvin. Calvin and his followers in the sixteenth century reflected a new belief in the importance of achievement and in the legitimacy of personal gain. The notion of "calling" changed from "a condition in which the individual is born [to] a strenuous and exacting enterprise to be chosen by himself and to be pursued with a sense of religious responsibility" (Tawney, p. 2). Success in work became identified as one of the signs of divine election, relieving any lingering, medieval fears that one might have been predestined to eternal damnation.

To be sure, there were qualities of austerity and altruism in the lifestyle of the "Protestant ethic." Wesley's advice was: "gain all you can, save all you can, *give all you can*" (emphasis added). This was an ethic of self-discipline if not self-denial. But the ethic was grounded in work and advancement: "gain all you can!"

Much has been written about the curious turn of logic, as well as events, by which followers of Jesus became advocates of material gain. One historian of this period, for example, cites a case in which medieval peasants were offered a higher piece rate as an inducement to harvest more: the more one harvested, the more one earned. Some peasants responded and did, indeed, step up the pace for higher wages. But others took the owner by surprise. As soon as they had earned the accustomed amount (according to the new scale, by harvesting less than before), they stopped working for the day. The latter group (who happened to be Catholics, untouched by the emerging Protestant work ethic) sought to earn whatever was required to support their familiar standard of life, and no more. That behavior might seem the more consistent with the teachings of Jesus. But the value of working to get ahead, the ethic of gain, had already begun to take hold.

An important part of this process has to do with human capacity. In *Good Work*, Peter Gillingham surveys the growth of creative enterprise in Western history. Not many centuries ago, Gillingham observes, only about one percent of the population was able to do more than maintain existing social systems. In this small minority were Aquinas, DaVinci, Erasmus, and other trailbreakers of our past. The other 99 percent suffered limited energy from poor diet, as well as limitations in education, communication, and other cultural resources.

At some time, presumably during the Renaissance (including the era of Calvin), with improved nutrition and increasing contact among cultures, the numbers of creative social innovators began to grow—from one to perhaps ten percent. These individuals found themselves in a position to specialize in particular skills and knowledge. They enjoyed, as Gillingham puts it, "an enormous sense of adventure, of excitement and liberation, at finally escaping the mire of the particular, the limited, the communal, the immediate, the local" (pp. 178, 79). The process by which the creative minority expanded was slow, to be sure. For example, at the time of the Declaration of Independence, nineteen of every twenty workers in America were engaged in agriculture (Friedman, p. xvii).

But in the industrialized countries, the process has been inexorable. Today, with improved nutrition and health care and education, with increased communication and contact with new technologies, more and more of us have what is required, intrinsically, to move up. Gillingham estimates that, in some parts of the world today, 30 to 40 percent of the population is prepared to take on roles of social leadership.

That revolution in human capacity appears today in many forms—at a general level, for example, in the often-unspoken assumption that each of us ought, somehow, to get ahead in his work. It is interesting to note, for example, that the term "success" originally meant something like the Spanish verb *suceder*, "to happen." The root meaning of success was simply the succession of events. The evolution of "success" into connotations of upward mobility reflects changing assumptions of our culture.

The assumption that one is "successful" only if rising higher sometimes appears in concerns for levels of compensation and title that can contradict an individual's essential aims in life.

> o Not long ago, I met with a man in his late forties who holds a master's degree in library science. Jack is a talented, if somewhat aimless, fellow whose career has come alive only in atmospheres of innovation. Once, in the army, he was stationed in Latin America as a teacher of English as a second language. The head of his unit was a young novelist who was engaged in writing what would become a Pulitzer Prize-winning book. The novelist often read from his work in progress; some of his characters could be recognized from real life. The whole setting was sparkled with creation.
>
> Another time, Jack traveled photographing babies in small-town department stores. The mothers of these infants, he recalls, were poor people who had little to celebrate; these photographs of their offspring probably would be among their most treasured possessions, inspiring dismal lives. Again, in telling of this job, his eyes lit up. He recalled how sensitive and inventive he had been, capturing bright expressions for the camera under pressures of time as the mothers and babies lined up in the store.

The Mirage of Perfect Work • **9**

By contrast, Jack's voice went dull when he told of a long period of employment as a university librarian. He actually had found that work monotonous, and hated it. But concern for status had kept him there for eight years, and impels him to seek another college-library job today. Introducing himself to strangers as a librarian felt good.

The assumption that success means moving up in one's work appears in clearest form today in the way we view academic credentials. The changing meaning of postsecondary education has been influenced in recent years by radical shifts in demographics. During the 1970s, the number of Americans aged eighteen to thirty-four (the customary years of entrance to the workforce) increased by one-third. This was the same decade when women entered the paid-labor force in unprecedented numbers. Our economy met, and largely absorbed, an immense wave of new workers.

But the value of academic credentials also was affected by the educational orientation of this group. During the 1950s and 1960s, college enrollments increased 300 percent, and the number of college graduates almost doubled. From the late 1960s to the late 1970s, enrollment increased another 184 percent. But now the effects of the increase began to show in the marketplace, as the earning gap between college graduates and others narrowed from 40 to 25 percent. And other effects of "overcredentialing" became apparent.

A recent survey of adult males in the state of California found that of every one thousand, forty-four were attorneys (Gillingham, pp. 183, 184). Nor is law the only overpopulated profession. A friend of mine was walking through Berkeley the other day. A nice-looking fellow came up to him and handed him a leaflet—not a political bill or petition, but an advertisement for his new dental practice!

Robert Petersdorf of the University of California School of Medicine in La Jolla writes in the *New England Journal of Medicine*, "We have too many doctors, particularly specialists, and we need to institute birth control." At present, Petersdorf says, about half of our medical-school graduates pursue advanced training in specialties, when the number of specialists actually needed is less than 20 percent. "To put it bluntly, there are just not enough patients to keep them all busy. In the communities with which I am familiar, there are few echocardiograms in search of cardiologists to read them, there is only a rare belch wanting a gastroenterologist, and there is not a single, even slightly plugged coronary that does not have three surgeons waiting in the wings. . . ." (*Denver Post*, October 27, 1983)

Overcredentialing is rampant in business education. Between 1964 and 1980, the number of MBAs awarded annually in the United States increased tenfold and the market, understandably, has been flooded (Kolbus, Fallows).

Ivar Berg's study *Education and Jobs: The Great Training Robbery* documents cases in which masses of workers earned advanced degrees only to discover, in a static economy, that their employers adapted to larger numbers of degree-holders by raising credential requirements for the same jobs. A position that formerly required a high school diploma now required an undergraduate degree; a bachelor's degree, a master's; and so on. Even more serious complications confront those whose degrees outstrip the level of their experience. An MBA or CPA without equivalent work experience may have great difficulty securing any kind of employment.

To be sure, what one learns in an advanced-degree program may have substantial, intrinsic value—and market value as well—if one can keep his education and experience in synchrony. "Knowledge is the new wealth," says John Naisbitt in *Megatrends*, and in a broad sense I believe he is right. But the promotion of advanced academic credentials as a proven means of getting ahead professionally often is nothing more than the selling of hope. Our society is not adept at correlating educational programs with marketplace needs. And too many of our academic institutions—under financial duress as the large baby-boom cohort of those born between 1946 and 1964 passes the traditional college years of young adulthood—develop new academic programs for adults more on the basis of their marketability to prospective students than by the value of the programs to the students themselves.

Today in most countries of the world the chimerical credentials of higher education continue to hold out promise of movement beyond social maintenance into the ranks of prestige and innovation. A young friend of mine in rural Kenya—so far removed from the rest of the world that at age twenty-two he has never been to the capital city of his own country—my friend feels the influence of social mobility and status. Aaron's four brothers and sisters all have left the small family village. Two are in Nairobi, another in Mombasa, and one already has worked as a computer programmer in Yugoslavia and New Zealand. Aaron failed to pass his secondary school exams, and so he finds himself tending the family farm. He has plans to enroll at a nearby school for a refresher course, to take the exams again. Then perhaps he, too, will move away. But does he really want to move, I ask? If economically it were possible to do so, would he stay and run the farm? He ponders some of the expectations of his family and himself, and only then does he respond quietly, "I think I would stay."

It's hard to escape the sense of obligation to move upward into positions of higher status and more influence in society. But opportunities have diminished, and the image of achievement seems more and more a mirage.

AND INDIVIDUALISM . . .

A second feature of the mirage of perfect work also can be viewed historically. The age of expansion that we have discussed gave rise to a seventeenth century of radical autonomy. This was the era in England of the expatriate Pilgrims, of John Bunyan's *Pilgrim's Progress*, of George Fox and the Religious Society of Friends. It was a time when medieval systems of social organization and belief were coming asunder. In this age of deep spiritual isolation—a sense that each of us is essentially a pilgrim and a stranger upon the earth—persons more often began to seek the meaning of life in their work. Of course, in an expanding economy at a time of new-world colonization, the quest often was rewarded. For the one percent who became the ten percent of those who were able to do more than maintain existing social systems, there were persuasive reasons for seeking personal identity and meaning in one's career.

Today, most of us take the values of individual mobility and career autonomy for granted. Sometimes it is helpful to remember that there are other ways to look at life based on alternative values—such as one's extended family. For example, I have seen a whole family of Hispanics move from rural New Mexico to the suburbs of Denver, determined to move collectively in order to continue a community they were therefore able to preserve. But however worthwhile, that's a minority view. Most of us measure ourselves as individuals.

Ironically, our investment in individualism has led to a new quest for community at work. The prospect of meeting social needs through work seems to have acquired increased significance in recent years, as nuclear family ties have become more tenuous. Sigmund Freud, in an oft-quoted comment, observed that two marks of human maturity were the abilities to love and to work (*lieben und arbeiten*). Today, the arena for both activities often turns out to be the workplace. For many, that is one of the few remaining, reliable sources of community. Social pollster Daniel Yankelovitch reports in his book, *New Rules*, that interest in his questions reflecting "search for community" showed an increase of 50 percent during the past few years. He notes, further, that between 1960 and 1980, while the number of "single households" increased 66 percent, the percentage of Americans who preferred living in an ongoing, monogamous relationship remained constant at 96 percent (Yankelovitch, pp. 96, 249).

Those figures reflect a painful discrepancy, which I often hear expressed by clients. The other day, a young woman who has worked hard in several jobs that didn't last and who now is in the first stages of divorce, spoke of her wish to find "an organization that will love me back." In Studs Terkel's book, *Working*, Barbara Terwilliger observes:

> Human beings must work to create some coherence. You do
> it only through work and through love. And you can only
> count on work.   (Terkel, p. 424)

It is probably this complex of needs to find community and
build friendships through the workplace that accounts for the
large stake many people have there. Harvey Brenner, a sociologist at Johns Hopkins University, noted that a one percent rise
in unemployment results in a 4.1 percent rise in suicide, a 5.1
percent rise in homicide, and a 1.9 percent rise in mortality. (*Rocky
Mountain News*, July 21, 1983) Another study, of chief executive
officers in New York City, reports that these CEOs lived an
average of only eighteen months after retirement. A poll of *Los
Angeles Times* readers, asked whether they would continue to
work if they could afford not to, found that 70 percent would remain on the job.

That is one reason why work today is so important—why in
all our ambivalence and frustration with it, we will not give up
the search to find fellowship in what we do. It is the point of John
Naisbitt's observation:

> Because we want to be with each other, I don't think many of
> us will choose to work at home in our electronic cottages. . . .
> Very few people will be willing to stay home all of the time and
> tap out messages to the office. People want to go to the office.
> People want to be with people, and the more technology we
> pump into the society, the more people will want to be with
> people.   (*Megatrends*, pp. 45–46)

That's why so many Americans are reluctant to give up on their
careers, even at a time when both in quality and quantity work
is likely only to decline. When one looks around for a place to
center one's life in meaningful community, it's hard to find an
alternative.

. . . AND THE POTENTIAL OF NEW TECHNOLOGY
The third feature of the mirage of perfect work is part of a changing view of technology. Technology essentially is nothing more
than a way of getting something done. All human societies in

this sense are technological. But consider some recent advertisements:

- The thin young man trots out of a thick fog, and peers into the camera. What first appeared a malformation of the head turns out to be a helmet. The young man is a soldier. "Technology is taking over the world," he warns. "Keep up with it, or you'll be left behind!" In the scenes that follow, the young soldier targets from a tank; the targets are displayed in computer graphics. At the end, having learned a presumed marketable skill, he vows not to be left behind. "Be all that you can be! Find your future in the Army!"
- Data General television commercials for portable computers display military leaders from the past suddenly confronted by new weapons—the catapult and the cannon. Horses bolt, warriors recoil in fear, as the sobering question sounds: "Are you buying yesterday's technology?"
- *The Sharper Image Catalog*, displaying new electronic gadgets, features Roger Moore's James Bond on the cover, pistol in hand. Moore's 007 film, *A View to a Kill*, is publicized, and the catalog of new technology is subtitled: "007 guide to equipping the elite secret agent."

The promotion of new technology on the basis of fear and combat rests on two assumptions that have become deeply ingrained in our culture. The first is that technological advance is a good thing, that the environment on which our technology acts is, and ought to be, capable of alteration. Daniel Boorstin, for example, in his provocative history of exploration, *The Discoverers*, lauds those who liberated mankind from dependence on the seasons by inventing first the nonlunar calendar, and then the clock. We in Western culture assume the value of those feats. But there are ancient cultures (in the Orient for example and the American Southwest) that embody other views. From those perspectives, the moon and everything else in nature are numinous. In transcending them, we are bound to suffer spiritual loss, for something in our environs is holy.

The second assumption is more recent. It is the notion that

technological competition is a good or, at any rate, necessary aspect of modern life. "Don't lose out! Don't get left behind! Don't be caught [in battle] with yesterday's technology!" That's technocracy—the view that technology rules the world.

Competition, of course, is not unique to contemporary times. Natives in ancient villages competed. But not with constantly changing devices. Technological competition-as-warfare is a relatively new idea, and a sorry one. In our culture it rests, I believe, on the other two features of the perfect-work mirage—the assumed values of growth and gain, and of individualism. If we learn to assume, as we have, that the meaning of life is to be found in our expansiveness as individuals, we are bound to seek whatever instrument of personal advantage we can find. And in that process we may find ourselves caught up in an unmanageable pace of change.

Much has been written of the rampant rate of technological change in our time. Alvin Toffler, in describing three pivotal points in the development of our culture, dates the agricultural revolution from 8000 B.C.; the industrial revolution from the end of the seventeenth century; and the postindustrial, electronic age from 1955. The decreasing time between phases is dramatic (Toffler, *The Third Wave*, p. 14).

In *The Micro Millennium*, the late British computer scientist, Christopher Evans, offered a graphic illustration of the exponential growth rate that is reflected in Toffler's data. If one should take a sheet of paper and fold it fifty times, forgetting the physical impossibility involved, that mutlifolded sheet would extent past the moon, beyond the orbit of the planet Mars, and into the asteroid belt! (p. 109).

The most serious impact of rapid technological change is on individual careers. Michael Crichton in *Five Patients* relates one example taken from medical history. In 1846, the noted surgeon Robert Liston performed the first operation in England using anaesthesia. It was the second such operation in history, and it was a success. The anaesthesia worked, and Liston amputated his patient's leg in exactly 28 seconds (pp. 89, 90). But whereas surgical speed not long ago had meant a great deal when operating on a patient who was conscious, with anaesthesia the skill was immediately obsolescent. The similar outdating of skills is far more prevalent today, and we fear it. "Technology is taking over the world! Don't get left behind!"

With the emergence of the electronic age, the phenomenon of obsolescent skills has been compounded by cybernation—the automation of tasks formerly performed by human workers. This process and its consequent efficiency already can be seen in blue-collar manufacturing jobs, where productivity of workers supported by robots recently has almost doubled. There is every indication, as we shall see, that white-collar occupations (where during the same period productivity rose less than five percent) will be next (Norman, passim).

There is a school of thought that holds the job loss becoming so endemic today is simply a passing phase. Some theorists point out that every historic instance of technological progress has given rise to protests by workers who feared the loss of their jobs. So, for example, in early nineteenth-century England, the Luddites smashed textile machines. They were proven wrong, their fears groundless, as the new technology gave rise to new occupational roles in the expanded economy that the new machines made possible. John Naisbitt identifies several stages in the introduction of new technology and suggests that we are still in the earliest phase of computer applications, when the new technology is being applid to existing tasks. In *Megatrends* and in a commencement address at the University of Denver, June 1985, he has noted, for example, that the information-based "new economy" accounted for four million new jobs in the United States last year, and another three million the year before. We have not yet begun to see the plethora of new jobs that computer technology will make possible.

It would be comforting to accept that view, if for no other reason than that so many of the jobs eliminated by automation are rather dreadful occupations. I've never worked on an oil rig and, from the stories I've heard from clients, am sure I don't want to. A crew deep in slime and muck grapples with drilling bits on shifts around the clock, in a high wind at forty below, somewhere sixty miles northwest of Last Chance, Wyoming. Those are the stories they tell.

One of my clients is part of a group that has invented an automated-drilling rig; robots do all the dirty work. But the crew size is reduced from eight to one. Seven jobs (miserable jobs to be sure, but nonetheless jobs) have been eliminated. Will those jobs reappear in other forms—perhaps in related areas, such as building the automated rig, servicing it, adapting it to new purposes? There are persuasive reasons to doubt it. For one thing, new technology is being applied in radical ways. Robots are manufacturing robots. For another, productivity in many fields continues to increase even as the number of jobs declines. American agriculture is the classic case. At the time of the American Revolution, as we have noted, 95 percent of American workers were engaged in agriculture. Now the figure is something like four percent. And in the process agricultural productivity has mushroomed!

Labor economists call this phenomenon "jobless growth." There are strong indications that the process will not be confined to economic activities important in the past, such as agriculture and manufacturing. Jobless growth will be no less pervasive in the postindustrial society of the future.

Hank Koehn of Security Pacific Bank observes: "the economy shift to high tech information and services may increase productivity, profitability and economic growth, but this does not necessarily mean more employment." He comments on two areas of presumed employment growth in the new economy:

> There is . . . the projection that systems analysts will be in great demand. I would suggest that was part of the past. We are entering the era of the user with computer systems. We do not need further systems analysts to accompany the increase in computer use. The Bureau of Labor Statistics also says that we need computer maintenance workers. That is clearly ridiculous to me. We do need some. But as the price of the machines drops and the mean time to failure increases, when the thing fails we will throw it out. . . .
>
> Financial services is a growth industry, according to projec-

tions of the 1980s and the 1990s. But will it provide employment? In 1982 there were 480,000 bank tellers in the United States. There were also 35,721 automated teller machines (ATMs) performing three billion financial transactions. Fifteen thousand ATMs were installed in 1983 and that number will more than double this year. Why would there be an increase in the clerical force of the banking community in the decade ahead? It is clearly absurd that there will be. (pp. 2, 3)

For the duration of the future I can see, you and I will live in an economy marked by jobless growth. Sometimes the phenomenon will be hidden, as when the defense industry is used to create jobs and take up the slack. Willis Harmon writes: "Much of the problem [of unemployment] has been concealed; for example, it seems apparent that the US economy since the 1930s has been able to maintain a politically acceptable level of employment only by preparing for war and by becoming arms supplier to the world (a role which Americans harshly criticized Germany for playing over a half century ago)" (p. 102).

Similarly, the reality of jobless growth also may be screened by demographic imbalance. In the commencement address cited above, Naisbitt noted that next year (as the baby-boom cohort ages) the numbers of new entrants to the labor force in the United States will begin a period of decline that will last through the remainder of this century. That may be good news for the graduates of 1985, the tail end of the crowded cohort. But the university faculty in attendance was to be reduced by 20 percent during the next two years, as their school struggled to maintain viability in the face of declining numbers of prospective young-adult students. The good news for one age group may be bad for another.

Furthermore, the fact that fewer young Americans will enter the labor force pales before burgeoning population in other parts of the world. Half the people in Africa are under fifteen years of age (Lamb, p. 16). In Mexico, about 75 percent of the population is less than twenty-five-years old. By the end of this century the number of prospective, new workers in developing countries will be five times those in industrialized nations, according to "The Unemployment Time Bomb " (chart number 37 in *The New*

State of the World Atlas). Where will all those young people find work?

To be sure, we ought not to underestimate the prospects of new economic growth and the possibilities of responding more effectively to change as, for example, through occupational retraining. We will explore some of those approaches in subsequent chapters. But we need to view such developments realistically, in the context of what is in fact a new age where growth will have limits.

People from many parts of the world are seeking a new perspective on the place and meaning of work in their lives. Sally Sadler, writing from Brussels in the Quaker Council for European Affairs publication *Around Europe* (July/August 1983), describes a special session of the European Parliament on the problem of unemployment: currently at 11 percent in Europe. Some of the proposals raised in the meetings seemed positive: increased job sharing, more investment in training, and better methods of determining and communicating workers' skills.

But in the final analysis, she says, the proposals of the European Parliament seem set upon the same mirage we've scrutinized in this chapter.

> Illusions that the recession will go away, that there will be a return to the "full employment" of the '60s seemed to be the basis of many of the Parliament's proposed solutions. The employment situation was discussed almost exclusively in terms of economic models and social values which belong to the period of the industrial revolution.

Those of us who hope to live fully and contribute effectively to our time need to look critically at conventional images such as the mirage of perfect work. We need a new vision of work. And we need to learn new ways of involving ourselves in employment with others, working through the promise and challenge of our changing times.

The next two chapters probe two features of personal growth toward employment as involvement: faith and productivity. They lead to an extensive description of how workplaces are found.

CHAPTER 2

RE-ENVISIONING WORK

We are living through the closing chapters of the established and traditional ways of life. We are in the beginnings of a struggle, which will probably last for generations, to remake our civilization. . . . It is a time for prophets and leaders and explorers and inventors and pioneers and for those who are willing to plant trees for their children to sit under.

Walter Lippmann

In *Between Man and Man*, Martin Buber observed that all of human history can be understood as alternating epochs of habitation and homelessness (p. 126). Studies of adult development confirm that this process of rooting and relocation occurs in the lives of individuals as well. In every life, there come times when established assumptions, through which we have viewed the world and organized our lives, come asunder. The assumptions are questioned and finally seen as something like mirages, distortions of reality rather than reliable guides. Yet, the process of moving forward may not come easy. Having settled down in a comfortable environment, which we felt we would never leave, we may be loath to give it up.

○ Greg looks like a typical undergraduate. Blond shaggy hair, ski vest, jeans with a hole exposing an entire knee. He stops by my office to inquire about our alumni career services. Greg's problem is that, while he looks like an undergraduate, he isn't. He graduated two years ago, and has spent the intervening time tending bar and skiing in a mountain-resort town. At length, it occurred to him that he ought to look for a permanent job, and he's been having difficulty finding one. I suggest that he begin with a series of vocational interest tests. Greg is enthusiastic; he'd like to take the tests tomorrow. But he has some difficulty in scheduling them. For you see, he confides, tonight his fraternity is having its seasonal beer blast, and he can't let the brothers down. The career counseling will have to wait since Greg plans to spend tomorrow hung over!

○ Don first decided to become a geologist in the eighth grade. His dad brought home a book on the subject and, for some reason, he became hooked on rocks. He completed a college major and then a graduate degree in uranium geology and developed a successful career in the field.

Then came the accident at Three Mile Island, and public disenchantment with nuclear power. The field of uranium geology began to crumble. One after another, Don's colleagues were laid off. Some were offered jobs unrelated to their training. Others, who were mobile, continued their careers overseas. Don's wife has her own career, though, and his kids are established in school here; so he chose to stay. Last week, the notice that he had been dreading finally arrived. Don's department will be closed. His career as uranium geologist is over.

Change always has carried the threat of the unknown, and human beings have a long history of resisting it. Medieval geographers and theologians retarded the exploration of new worlds for centuries by their reluctance to use the ancient term *terra incognita* to describe places on their maps where Westerners had not been. It was more comforting to define the limits of the world on the basis of unfounded speculation than to face the fact that a good part of the world actually was unknown (Boorstin, p. 82ff.).

Jesus once came upon a man lying crippled beside the famed Jerusalem pool of healing, Bethesda. He had lain on his pallet, he said, for thirty-eight years, waiting with others for an intermittent spring to move the waters. Local tradition held that one who lay in the waters when the spring was active could be healed. Jesus' response to the man's request for help in getting closer to the pool was not what he expected. "Rise!" he said. "Take up your bed and walk!" (Mark 2:09).

Earlier Biblical prophets took a similar stance when confronted with traditional wisdom. From Elijah facing the priests of Baal on, the prophets were radical critics of honored views inherited from the past. Their role in ancient Hebrew culture was based on two distinctive functions: *seeing* in the sense of discernment (in Hebrew, *roeh*), and *active proclamation* (in Hebrew, *nabi*) of what they saw.

The Biblical prophets were accustomed to look beneath the surface of contemporary events to search out the deep, underlying currents that shaped them. Elijah pondered the meaning of a famine, Jeremiah the significance of shifting political alliances, Isaiah the death of a king. All of them struggled to understand the meaning of confusing, current events.

And the prophets took action on the basis of what they saw. Each of them so identified with his message that he tried to embody it. From Elijah's perilous trial on Mount Carmel to Jesus' costly decision to re-enter Jerusalem, the prophets all identified personally with their interpretation of current happenings and then acted accordingly.

Traditionally, of course, prophetic discernment and action are behaviors that can be expected only from a small "Abrahamic minority." Most people, in ancient Israel as in other societies, could be expected to respond to the future only when challenged or goaded into creative and responsible action. Ordinarily they would act by the norms. Alternative visions and ventures into the unknown were for a few prophetic specialists.

Today, in a welter of confusing and sometimes distressing economic and social conditions such as jobless growth, there is increasing evidence that social conformism can be dysfunctional. The behaviors that many of us have learned to honor, as in seeking the perfect job, fail to provide the rewards we were promised. "Stay in school! Work hard to get ahead! Dress for success! Follow the rules!" Increasingly it makes more sense to reconsider traditional wisdom and get up from the pool.

The process by which we move forward that way into the future has been conceived and described in many ways. The ancient Chinese used the term *tao* that (just as the Hebrew, *Torah*) we translate "way." In Chinese, *tao* was both noun and verb. They could think of "waying" as a process of following/creating a path.

"Faith" is a Biblical term for that process, and it ought to be a verb as well: like "journey," or "venture." Faith is a process of configuring and creating the future through our actions. It is a much more fully human way into the future than, for example, autonomically acting out scripts of the past. But faith requires courage: the willingness to acknowledge the terra incognita quality of what we do not know, and the capacity to invest ourselves in a future whose substance may not yet be apparent. The author of the book of Hebrews in the Bible describes the process this way: "Now faith is the assurance of things hoped for, the conviction of things not seen." Abraham and those who followed his example "went out, not knowing where he was to go. By faith he sojourned in the land of promise, as in a foreign land." Abraham, and his followers, "all died in faith, not having received what was promised, but having seen it and greeted it from afar, and having acknowledged that they were strangers and pilgrims on the earth" (Hebrews 11).

Faith celebrates the unknown. In the spirit of faith, one actually can appreciate the unknown wilderness in our human experience. Perhaps the naturalist Eliot Porter went a bit far in proclaiming that "in wilderness is the preservation of the world." But it is evident that without the contingency of uncharted land, terra incognita, the process of making/finding one's way would be impossible and life would lose some of its zest and meaning. Human life is most fully human when we face the challenge of finding a way through the wilderness of the unfamiliar.

The life of faith always includes an element of belief. We move ahead through the unknown, encouraged by an image of the life we seek there. Our survival through periods of transition is supported by our image of arrival on the other side. But Biblical faith always must be distinguished from any sort of creed or sanctioned belief. Faith is purposeful movement toward a future that one can envision, but never possess. While faith entails a measure of finality in the sense of concern with ultimate human issues, finality does not reside in the certitude of one's vision. In the life of faith, one never has "the last word." In *The Finality of Faith*, the late theologian Nels Ferre put it well:

> To have finality of faith does not mean having the final answers. Whoever knows all the answers has no faith. What he has is knowledge. The finality of faith, on the contrary, involves *not* knowing final answers. The finality of faith expresses the truth that faith is final, not as knowledge but as faith on the move toward finding.   (p. 3)

But if faith cannot be encapsuled in traditional creeds, that is not to say it is without content. Biblical faith, as Ferre put it, is "invitation to pilgrimage." The life of faith finds substance at the boundaries of growth. As each of us finds a way through the uncharted wilderness that surrounds us, we encounter certain contingencies, barriers in the path ahead. And our journey in faith finds definition there. Faith lives most fully in the promise and threat of the next frontier.

Today many of our most critical frontiers are global. We live in an age of exceptional hazard, confronting international issues that overshadow our troubled national economy even as they impact it. These global problems have serious, long-range consequences and profound implications for employment. For example:

- The United States, with about 5 percent of the world's population, consumes almost 40 percent of the world's resources every year. The industrial pollution and environmental destruction (such as deforestation) required by that kind of consumption are significant factors in the expected extinction of 15 to 20 percent of all the species on earth (half a million to two million) by the end of this century, as well as the accumulation of hazardous nuclear wastes whose half-life is approximately five times as long as the period of recorded history (*Global 2000*, p. 37).

- The proliferation of nuclear weapons continues to grow exponentially; in ten years, the number of countries capable of building them is likely to increase fivefold. In the United States, six million workers are employed in a defense industry that contributes little to the nation's productivity even as it supports the insanity of international arms escalation.

- Military expenditures, worldwide, average one million dollars every minute; and the percentage of expenditure is highest in the poor, developing countries that can afford it least. "The total of world military expenditures is approaching six hundred billion dollars per year, most of [it] spent by the Soviet Union and the United States. Annual world expenditures for development aid are about twenty billion dollars" (Willens, p. 92).

- The income gap between industrialized and "developing" nations is widening. Our government ranks seventeenth among the world's developed nations in percentage of Gross National Product devoted to foreign aid (Willens, p. 86). Worldwide population is expected to grow even faster at the end of this century than today, with 90 percent of the increase in the poorest countries (*Global 2000*, p. 1).

Discomforting as they are, circumstances such as these can be seen as frontiers—invitations to pilgrimage or, as the early Quakers would say, "openings." From this point of view, we may see new possibilities for employment as involvement in the world.

A shift in view which enables us to view hazardous difficulties as creative challenge—employment, for example, as the opportunity for involvement—is a catalyst of faith. Some people by nature seem to see life this way.

One of my clients, who could laugh at a time when his luck was down, said that he could identify with the little boy who visited a farm for the first time. His parents let him go off to explore and found him several hours later hip deep in a pile of horse manure, shoveling steadily. "Why in @#*%! are you doing that?" they cried. "Well," he replied, resting on his shovel, "somewhere in here there's gotta be a pony!"

Most of us are less sanguine, and more reluctant to "dig in." But many of us can recall moments when we saw life in a new light and discovered some basis for venturing forward in faith. For me, such occasions are sporadic, and usually occur when I am up against my limits and open to new learning.

Several years ago we had the opportunity of spending a few weeks in rural western Kenya at a meeting of the Friends World Committee for Consultation. That was to be a remarkable gathering of people from all parts of the world. We expected an adventure, but nothing like what happened.

We arrived in Kenya shortly after an abortive coup that we learned of en route, and found the country under military occupation. The streets of Nairobi were strewn with broken glass from looting, much like Chicago in the 1960s. The morgue overflowed with several-hundred bodies of those killed in the conflict. In the city, we lived under curfew. On the way to our conference center, deep in the back country, thirty miles from Lake Victoria, our buses were stopped and searched repeatedly. Once there, we peaceful Quakers found the center guarded by several dozen local militia bearing automatic rifles. We never knew why or from whom we were being guarded. Other elements of life in a new continent—drums from the jungle, strange noises in the night—provided what educators call a "teachable moment."

I recall two personal lessons in particular. A group of Japanese Friends had brought two films on the effects of atomic radiation on individuals who had "survived" the attacks on Hiroshima and Nagasaki. The films were horrifying, and I especially remember a Kenyan woman in full traditional dress walking out of the auditorium in tears. Some time that evening, I became fully convinced that, whatever differences exist in cultures, all human beings are essentially one.

My other lesson came from a talk by Simeon Shitemi, a Kenyan government official who had been educated in Quaker institutions in his country and later in the United States. Shitemi had served as his nation's chief delegate to the United Nations, and some of his insights on the military arms race from the point of view of the Third World were profound. But what I remember most was his gentle, offhand comment of four words: "We'll work it out!"

"We'll work it out!"? Under any other circumstances, from almost anyone else, I'd have dismissed that kind of statement in an instant. But in those surroundings, in the presence of an exceptionally diverse group of spiritually sensitive people, I really heard him, and took heart. And I pondered the possible truth in what he said. Maybe we *will* "work it out." I have considered the possibility, for example, that stationed where we are in a long, evolutionary process whose foreseeable outcome does not look good, perhaps we face a common frontier. It may be, I sometimes imagine, that we are living in an epoch such as Walter Lippman described, and that if we are truly alive to this time we might have the opportunity to learn some lessons, such as how to deal with conflict creatively and how to share—lessons that will turn out to be pivotal in the long, slow course of Creation. And if that is so, surely I have a part to play!

Of course, I don't feel that way all the time. I am as capable of cynicism, selfishness, and despair as anyone I know. But the life of faith and the sense that there is some purpose in this journey are sporadically reawakened. And then the contingencies of life show up as frontiers that, addressed in faith, open new vistas for our humanity. We may find, in the words of Pogo, some "inescapable opportunities."

Nowhere does the frontier manifest itself more clearly than in the exigencies of employment—our involvement in the world. The issues that we confront today in relation to work involve us not only with the great, collective challenges of life in global communities, but also with contingencies of our personal lives— as we seek our part in that big picture. It is my experience that, as we identify and encounter individual boundaries, each of us may find opportunities to venture ahead in faith in ways that, ultimately, benefit everyone. Helping individuals to discover those passages is a constant source of stimulation and challenge in my own work.

> o Sometimes the frontier is clearly geographic. Marv was a successful attorney when I worked with him. His parents, survivors of the Holocaust, had emigrated from Germany to four countries before settling in Detroit. Marv learned from them, I sensed, something about the process of moving ahead in the face of adversity.
>
> Marv experienced a setback of his own after he graduated from college. He did poorly on qualifying exams for law school and was not admitted. He did find an opportunity to work in campus fund raising for a national Jewish organization and enjoyed that work for several years. Finally, he completed law school while working in a lawn-care business he and a friend established. He then built a practice in Atlanta. Marv married a woman who shared his commitment to Judaism, and they and their children were able to spend several vacations in Israel. The country grew on them and, after a year in a kibbutz, Marv and Emily decided to put their house on the market and emigrate to Israel as permanent residents.

Marv's purpose in coming to me was to explore occupations he might pursue in Israel. He recognized that his legal training would not transfer directly to another culture, and that now there were other factors to consider—a language barrier, the possible value of his small business experience, how best to meet his needs and those of his new country through his professional life.

I never learned the direction he took, once in Israel. But, seeing his enthusiasm and his awareness of an evolving life purpose, I never worried about his success. Long ago, Marv had learned how to address frontiers and venture in faith.

o Other frontiers are within us. Paul is a thirty-five-year-old geophysicist. He completed college as a physics major in the early 1970s, on a campus filled with unrest. His academic record was as unstable as the school. One semester he made straight A's, the next he spent in political organizing and almost flunked out. Later, while working in oil exploration, Paul finished a master's degree, and excelled in the program. He went on to specialize in the application of electrical methods to mineral exploration, and invented a new mathematical technique that helped make that process possible.

His success, however, was not to last. Gradually, Paul realized that he had entered the mineral exploration field during a boom period, when temporary shortages and speculation were spurring competitive and domestic exploration projects. When he lost his full-time job, Paul became an independent consultant; then the consulting dried up and he began to face the reality of unemployment. His highly specialized training in geophysical exploration and geology seemed nontransferable to other fields and he spent many months agonizing over polite rejection letters.

We worked together to establish a program of interviewing among physicists and computer specialists in fields outside geology, looking for a place where Paul could transfer and build on his existing skills. In talking with these colleagues, Paul was reminded of the unevenness of his education. In some areas, he was a recognized innovator; in others, as an undergraduate in the 1970s, he was embarrassingly deficient.

Finally, a job turned up with a research group in Albuquerque. The position carried much lower salary and status than any he'd had in the past ten years. On the face of it, the job was a demotion. In addition, the laboratory worked primarily on defense contracts; that didn't sit well with Paul's political values. But the job offered an opportunity to grow professionally in important ways. Paul could review some of the material he'd failed to learn in college and branch out in the expanding field of atmospheric electromagnetic research at a time when geology continued to decline.

Recently I saw Paul again, and reviewed his short- to long-range goals through a skills-based résumé we had developed earlier. I was impressed. Paul had begun to identify specific learning objectives on the job, in both physics and computer science, through which he could become more marketable as a physicist. In addition, he was exploring a path that eventually could lead him back to geophysics—a field he still misses. An associate at the lab who specializes in constructing equipment had offered to help Paul build an electromagnetic receiver for a fraction of the retail cost. The receiver could be used for some independent exploration of mineral deposits, both as a pleasant weekend activity in the mountains with friends and as a possible future source of income should they find themselves in a position to stake their own claims. He also intended to explore geological applications of some of the new, computer-supported modeling techniques used by research physicists.

In a few years, as existing energy sources decline, Paul expects to see new opportunities for exploration geophysicists. With knowledge of transferable techniques from atmospheric physics and with his own electromagnetic receiver, Paul hopes one day to find himself working as an independent consultant, back on the frontiers of geophysics. He plans to continue regular interviews with a broad range of colleagues in geophysics, atmospheric physics, and computer science, and to update the skills-summary paragraphs of his résumé as a way of monitoring his progress.

That process is complex, especially for someone like Paul with highly specialized skills. Yet it's a highly promising process for those of us who, living in the midst of social change, hope to build creative careers in fields we care about.

In chapter 4 we'll review some techniques in the process of managing learning for career development. First, however, we'll look at some of the dynamics of productivity—the process through which people such as Marv, Paul, and the rest of us can venture toward employment on the next frontier.

CHAPTER 3

PRODUCTIVE WORK

The study on work quality came to mind not long after I had purchased a new automobile from Detroit. The car was attractive, and I often had admired its teardrop lines. It performed well on a test drive, and was American-made. I decided to buy the car: a snazzy, red hatchback.

The teardrop form, unfortunately, proved to be something of a portent. For, in the first few months of ownership, that car was to cause me heartbreak. Despite its fine design, the auto had been thrown together. Whoever had assembled the car had done so in a stupor. Door handles, visors, moldings, emergency brake handle all hung by a screw—and fell off as I drove the first few hundred miles. At twenty-thousand miles the clutch went out. At thirty-five thousand miles, the car and I appeared to share a tenuous sort of truce, a hiatus between costly repairs. But I was not encouraged. I spoke with a friend who is a parish minister. One of his parishioners, then an auto dealer, had sold him the same model. The dealer retired, and soon after took my friend aside. In a contrite spirit bordering on confession, the retired dealer apologized for ever having sold his minister that car. It was bound to come apart, he said; and it had.

The study I recalled was done by the University of Michigan. Researchers there had interviewed a broad cross section of American workers, asking them whether they would be willing to purchase the goods they made. Twenty-seven percent of the workers interviewed indicated that they would not be willing to buy what they had manufactured.

Quite often today, data such as these are cited in articles on the subject of "productivity." Economists note the steady decrease in our rate of productivity, and many include declining worker morale as a factor in that trend. Other commentaries document the same condition. Robert Half, head of a major employment firm, estimates that employees who deliberately waste time on the job cost our economy between 125 and 150-billion dollars a year. Industrial productivity is an important concern that sometimes touches us directly, as in my experience as a car owner. The worker who assembled part of the car, and the inspector who was to have passed on the quality of his work, had failed to function productively. For lack of skill and/or concern, they had not held up their end of our economic transaction.

But there is more to productivity than can be measured in the generation of goods and services, which is the objective definition of the term. Subjectively, as Erich Fromm noted, productivity has a somewhat deeper meaning: making full use of one's powers. It is not by accident that we use the same term to denote both processes. There is, indeed, a natural and inherent connection between living productively—experiencing and making full use of one's personal potential and powers—and the quality and quantity of what an individual produces in the economic arena. The first feature of productivity engenders the second.

A number of social critics have commented on the fate of productivity in our Western economic history. Centuries ago, in the agrarian age, production and consumption were closely linked. Most persons consumed a good part of what they produced, and they produced mainly for their own and their family's consumption. The industrial era changed all that. Production and consumption were split asunder, connected only by the uncertain medium of the "marketplace" (Toffler, *Wave*, p. 37ff. and passim).

With the division of production and consumption in the industrial age, another interesting development occurred. Methods of production became increasingly efficient, and the time required to produce necessary goods diminished. E. F. Schumacher suggested that in our society only about 3.5 percent of total "social time" is spent in production. Consequently, Schumacher noted, "The prestige carried by people in modern industrial society varies in inverse proportion to their closeness to actual production" (*Small*, p. 150). As Thorstein Veblen and others have noted, in the industrial era consumption acquired ever-greater status. "Consumption is the sole end and purpose of production," Adam Smith wrote at the beginning of that age. His view echoed through the "second-wave" centuries that followed. Today it sometimes seems that consumption has created a new work ethic of its own; frantic for the few jobs we can see, we virtually consume them.

That orientation to consumption underlies two common views of "full employment." Often we think of employment as full to the degree that our economy provides everyone with a job. Or we may measure our own employment by the standard of personal fulfillment; full employment is perfect work. Today, as we have seen, each of these assumptions may prove unrealistic and frustrating.

A better-founded view of full employment begins not with the consumption of work but with the personal aspect of production. If we regard employment essentially as involvement in the world, and productivity as the capacity to make full use of our powers, then we may ask how each of us can become more productive—more of who we potentially are. Full employment then can be understood as deep and distinctive participation in the world.

Viewing full employment as productive involvement can help us see the exigencies of finding paid employment from a larger perspective. Working for pay is but one avenue to productive involvement in the world. My clients who appear in case excerpts throughout this book are presented not so much as examples of successful job-seekers, but as persons who are struggling to become more productive. They are attempting to fulfill their human potential, some of my humanistic-psychologist friends would say. They are beginning to manifest "that of God in everyone," some of my Quaker Friends would say. In general, I believe that all of us are trying to become more fully who we are. Through employment, that quest involves us in the world.

Economists traditionally have identified several different components in the generation of goods and services and called them "factors of production." For an economy to function, they have found, certain prerequisites must be present: some *natural resources* such as land and a source of energy; *technology* capable of manufacturing what is needed; an adequate supply of *labor*; and concentrated support in the form of *capital*. John Kenneth Galbraith and others add factors such as *management* skills: the ability to coordinate complex relationships among these disparate elements.

The productivity of individuals can be understood in similar terms. For the capacity of any one of us to make something like full use of our human potential involves these same sorts of elements. At a time when established social systems are eroding around us, it seems especially important to understand these factors in relation to the lives of individuals: what is required for a person to become a productive human being?

The first factor of productivity (*see Figure 1*) is overlooked by many traditional economists. In the lives of individuals as of societies, motivation is primary. People become productive only when their lives find focus in some center of vitality and valuing. The Biblical idea of "soul," based on the Hebrew *nephesh*, reflects this view. Productive human life begins with "soul"—an animating, energizing vitality capable of infusing what we do with a sense of purposiveness and meaning. Closely related to vitality is some centered value—a sense of connection to sources of satisfaction and meaning in our lives. Productivity begins with a capacity to care about what we do.

FIGURE 1

FACTORS OF PRODUCTIVITY

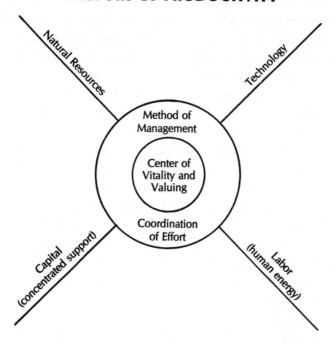

Richard Bolles has reminded us that the origin of another term parallels the concept of *nephesh*. "Enthusiasm" is derived from two Greek words, *en* (in) and *theos* (God). Genuine enthusiasm for what we do with our lives seems to involve participation in a deep realm of meaning in which some of us sometimes find the living presence of God. Together these concepts suggest the importance of motivation in productive living. What we do for a living follows from what we live to do.

How is it that persons discover this kind of motivation? How do we get in touch with our basic energies and values? Quakers speak of "centering down"—quieting, gathering, centering our impulses and energies to seek direction "as way opens." In seeking work, as anything else, each of us often is apt to act prematurely. We may run about in panic, responding in our stress to real or imagined fears. Not long ago I spoke with two colleagues in the field of adult education, both of whom have training and interests similar to mine. Both recently have lost their jobs. Those conversations were unsettling. What will happen to me? Am I next? Should I look for something more secure? Under the manifold stresses of widespread structural unemployment, it is easy for any of us to panic, to look for a life course based not on what we value but on what we fear.

It is helpful to remember that our predicament is not altogether new. Coping with panic and fear really is fundamental to the human condition. Elijah, in his anxiety after the traumatic trial on Mount Carmel, was overwhelmed by encounters with the tumult of earthquake, wind, and fire. Only after passing through that spiritual catacylsm did he experience the presence of God in a "still, small voice" (literally, "the sound of silence," Kings 1: 18ff.). The Gerasene demoniac, who said his name was "Legion, for we are many," was another representative human being, tormented by a multitude of needs and fears. Jesus, in caring for him, helped him to settle down and left him "clothed and in his right mind" (Mark 5).

The Taoists understood the importance of stillness and stressed a spirit of effortless activity, *wei wu wei*, "doing without doing."

> Thirty spokes will converge
> In the hub of a wheel;
> But the use of the cart
> Will depend on the part
> Of the hub that is void.
> > *Tao Te Ching*,
> > number 11,
> > R. B. Blakney translation

That image can integrate the "factors of productivity." Perhaps, when we live productively, our functioning is as a kind of wheel, supported by the several factors that contribute to productivity but centered in a "still point"—in the quiet coherence of our values.

Indeed the Wise Man's office
Is to work by being still
. . . quietness is master of the deed.
. . . High virtue is at rest.

Tao Te Ching,
numbers 2, 26,38

In each of these traditions, there is testimony to a fundamental process: working through our typical human encounters with panic, fear, and desperation to the point where one can experience quietude, gather one's concerns into conscious awareness, and center one's energies in a place of personal vitality and value. It is in a course of that kind that productive living begins.

The second concentric circle in the figure represents another important factor in productivity, whether at the individual or group level. Galbraith has noted that in large, complex organizations, the capacity to coordinate efforts is so critical that it ought to be regarded as one of the factors of production. The entire new profession of "management" derives from a recognition of this need. The same point can be made for the lives of individuals. The capacity to coordinate and manage one's activities is an important element in productive life.

The four axes in the figure correspond to classic "factors of production" in the economic life of societies: land, labor, capital, and technology. We'll look at them in turn.

The first is natural resources. All the elements of life in the biosphere, which advanced societies take for granted and which they often despoil, are basic to productivity. Many individuals think of this factor in relation to land; owning one's own home, for example, becomes an important aim in life. For others, particular concerns may emerge—the climate in which one functions best, for example. Productivity requires some involvement with natural resources.

Technology, as I have noted, simply signifies what we know how to do. Most of us have a few basic technical skills—such as typing and driving a car—and many of us find ourselves needing to acquire others. Classes in computer science, for example, are filled these days. The capacity to learn and relearn technical skills and to increase one's knowledge is a vital ingredient in productive living.

The factor of labor appears both in individual life as well as societal. Quite apart from our motivation and skill, how much energy does each of us actually have to produce what we care and know about? In recent years, leaders in the field of holistic health have taught us that health can transcend the absence of illness. Just as one can be more or less sick, so also one can be more or less well. High levels of wellness can contribute significantly to our productivity as individuals.

Finally, there is capital—usually in the form of money, although capital can take a great variety of forms. Capital is more than currency. John Naisbitt notes that capital was the most critical factor of production during the second wave, or industrial era. It replaced land, the essential feature in agrarian, first-wave civilization. Now, as Naisbitt maintains, technical skill and knowledge are paramount. That may be the case, but capital still appears important to individual productivity as a form of concentrated support. Capital is especially critical, of course, in the establishment of individual, entrepreneurial activities. Naisbitt notes that the rate of small business establishment in this country has increased about sixfold in the past few decades. To be sure, the great majority of these enterprises fail; but the rate of failure has remained constant, with more and more entrepreneurs succeeding. Capital is an important, if not sufficient, prerequisite to individual productivity, and especially vital to most entrepreneurial activity. But it is only one factor in productivity and ought not to be overvalued. Seldom have I met people who have found deep satisfaction in the mere accumulation of capital. A millionaire I met recently commented, "I have all the toys. Now what?" For most of us, money is an instrumental value—like jogging, important for the other things that it enables us to do.

When we view an individual in terms of productivity, it is useful also to consider how one person's productive life interacts with those of others. I have represented three alternative models of interaction in Figure 2.

The first is dependence: relations in the economic sphere that involve one or several persons in a relatively powerless, subordinate position with reference to some person in power. This is the assumed pattern of working life for many individuals. Whenever we seek a "job," offered by some larger employing organization, in effect we respond to this model. The relationships that follow are very similar to the economic dynamics of colonialism. In both instances, a powerful entity relates to satellite units in a top-down fashion. The large, parentlike organization provides its subordinates with sustenance, but at a considerable cost. For the individual units are required to produce only what the central entity requires. They interact with one another only through the parent body, with which they maintain a relationship of dependence. Whether we consider the economic life of the British Empire in the nineteenth century or the more recent traditional relationship of American workers to large employing companies, the structure is the same. It is a pattern that is changing markedly in our time as large employers become less and less significant as a source of jobs. (An MIT study found that 80 percent of new jobs in the United States in recent years were in firms that employed fewer than a hundred workers, and two-thirds in firms with fewer than twenty. That trend continues.)

A second form of economic life is independence. We have noted already the rising rate of small-business development. Independence has experienced corresponding growth as a societal value during the past decade. I often encounter it among individuals who have become disillusioned with their career paths within large institutions. Some of these people, having "topped out" or been "promoted to a broom closet," gravitate to new careers in which they work essentially on their own. Many of them become independent distributors, sell insurance, or engage in craft work. The desire of American workers for independence continues strong, supported by an ethic of self-fulfillment.

The career roles of the independent mode sometimes develop

FIGURE 2

RELATIONSHIPS WITH OTHERS

Dependence

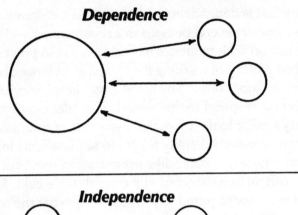

Independence

Interdependence

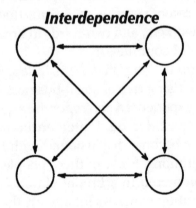

in reaction to the powerlessness one feels in dependence. One reason that 85 percent of new business ventures fail, I believe, is that so many of them are founded not on a solid basis of thoughtful planning, but rather on an impulse to escape one's employer.

Sometimes people who devote themselves to creating private workplaces get stuck there. There is a certain "Lone Ranger" quality, for example, among many independent businesspeople—a resistance to any kind of involvement with colleagues. Others, however, find it possible to translate the same concerns that led them to work alone into the collaborative mode of interdependence. This is true of many entrepreneurs who move from solitude to some kind of collegial life with others. Sometimes this occurs in corporate life. John Naisbitt's term "intrapreneur" describes the person who can be enterprising within an organization. Other entrepreneurs move beyond isolation through trade and civic associations, as noted above. Those who function essentially as prophets or as artisans may live and work in solitude. Or they may move to an interdependent mode by linking up with others who are similarly involved with the causes or crafts they love.

The rewards one experiences as an interdependent worker are similar to what one receives in any shared relation. Skills are built; insights and enthusiasm grow. Both parties gain more than they invest. That is the point of Jesus' parable of the talents, I believe. It is only as we share what we have to offer, rather than hoard or protect it, that our gifts engender life.

But sharing leaves us vulnerable, and therein lies the risk of interdependence. For as interdependent workers (lovers, etc.), we rely upon the systems of our interaction. If we are less helpless than those who at an earlier stage must depend on others to give them jobs, we are, nonetheless, reliant on our colleagues. Should the system through which we are bound to them break down, we are left exposed. And the broader the span of our relationships and concerns, the more tenuous the system and the greater our threat of exposure. So, in the full mutuality of interdependence, there are risks no less than rewards.

Ultimately, however, most people find that productive life requires other people, and they begin to seek those kinds of relationships. This pattern is found, for example, among multilevel marketers such as Amway dealers or insurance agents, who may become far more enthused about relationships they are forming with one another in marketing/sales support organizations than about the process of selling their products. A number of these organizations seem to have taken on the character of virtual extended families, gathering for rallies, conferences, and even vacations together. I find that most persons, once having attained something like independence, do seek new relationships of interdependence just as developing nations, once freed from colonial dependence, and having passed through a period of precarious independence, may mature in the direction of more interdependent economic and cultural life. As E. F. Schumacher noted, there is a "multiplier effect" that accompanies interdependent economic activity. When individuals or groups are able to transcend dependence upon some powerful, parental other, and when they are able to move beyond the anxious isolation of independence, they may arrive at a point where free interdependence becomes possible. As talents once buried are unearthed and exchanged, a healthy synergy is born. Freely exchanging what each one brings to the marketplace, there is growth in productivity. And the sum far surpasses its parts.

How is this process engendered? Certainly it is possible to argue that some forms of economic and political organization encourage interdependent productivity more than others do. Any system that denies individual initiative, such as totalitarian Communism; or that consigns persons or groups to narrow, limited roles such as colonialism; or that subordinates all other human capacities to the accumulation of material goods, such as classical capitalism—any of these systems inhibits the development of productive interdependence. One might envision a social system that would promote interdependent productivity, as Schumacher did. But of course that would be only a vision, for that kind of economic system really doesn't exist.

In the last analysis, productivity is an opportunity and responsibility of individuals. It requires a pilgrimage that each of us must make alone.

o I first met Karen about three years ago. She attended a meeting to learn about our new career development program for alumni, and then called me the next morning to indicate she thought she'd invest in the program and enroll. We began working together in a process of vocational interest assessment.

Of the hundreds of clients with whom I had done this kind of assessment process, I had encountered no one with a more confused, incongruous background than Karen. A quiet, sensitive person, she held an undergraduate degree in physical therapy and had worked in that field for fifteen years. Work was readily available, but she hated it. At first I couldn't understand why; she cared about helping people, liked working with her hands, and had excellent training. Why did she so dislike being a physical therapist? A great deal of it had to do with the hierarchy of medical institutions. She found her position confining, always under the direction of physicians. I was to understand a bit more about her feelings months later when I learned that her father, an intimidating figure to Karen, is a prominent local hospital administrator. At any rate, the profession of physical therapy clearly did not fit her needs.

Several years ago, convinced that she needed an alternative career, Karen enrolled in a master's degree program in anthropology. She completed the degree with great success, even publishing some articles in the field, but then determined that, should she earn her doctorate, the tight academic job market offered no prospects for employment. She returned to the despised position of physical therapist.

Karen and I reviewed a number of interest tests and values-clarification exercises. Nothing clear emerged. Noting her high interest in some kind of academic life, I suggested that she simply thumb through a catalog of graduate courses and see what struck her eye. She did this at home, and found herself drawn almost immediately to the field of speech communication. Karen talked a bit about her interest in speech. As a child she had been even more shy than she is today. She suffered from what people in the field call "communication apprehension," especially in front of large groups. Karen recalled one memorable incident in which she'd had to be carried off the stage when she froze up during a presentation in a school program. Karen cared a great deal about speech communication. She decided to enroll in some doctoral courses in communication, supporting herself by tolerable doses of physical therapy.

Recently I saw her again. Karen was quiet as ever, but animated. She had a kind of glow about her. She had completed a couple of speech courses and in the midst of one had found some work being done in the area of intercultural communication. That interested her, and she had written a paper about some of the communication problems encountered by Japanese and Americans in business. The subject involved her once again in anthropology, and she did a fine job. The paper was circulated among a number of faculty members in the schools of speech communication and business. Later, she asked my help in preparing another résumé, for a part-time job teaching nonverbal communication to employees of a local firm involved in international trade. She didn't yet see exactly how her interests would take form in a specific career, but she had found focus; she was onto something. Karen was emerging from the shadow of domination by her father's profession, out of dependence; she was venturing out from the isolation of private studies in a field where there is no place for her, out of independence; she was becoming involved with a group of colleagues and clients who share her concerns about improving communication and who welcome the particular gifts she brings to their field. She was venturing into the realm of interdependence.

Once functioning interdependently in the new field, Karen progressed farther. She was treating a fellow's knee at the health spa where she still works part-time as a physical therapist. Somehow Karen and the patient got into a conversation about school, and she told him about her hopes to work in the area of intercultural-business communication. The patient turned out to be a local official in the US Department of Commerce. Two weeks later, he'd helped place her in a paid internship conducting market research to support new ventures in international trade. Karen had moved another step toward her goal.

None of this is easy. Karen says quietly that she feels as though she is walking on eggshells. But her eyes sparkle as she says this, and it is impossible not to see that she is moving forward. There is an integration taking place, of her technical skills in anthropology and human service, and of her concern for problems of communication about which she has good reason to care. And as all of those elements begin to cohere, to come together in whatever employment she will find, Karen is venturing toward involvement in a life of growing productivity.

PART II

Finding a Workplace

INTRODUCTION

We have looked at the landscape of our working lives from a number of viewpoints. Sifting through some questionable assumptions about fulfillment and success, we have considered work in the context of productivity: making full use of our powers. We have explored faith as the human capacity to venture purposefully beyond the customary and the known. Now we must deal with pragmatics, considering some of the dynamics of finding meaningful employment.

How do people grow in productivity? How can we realize more of our creative potential, collaborating to address some of the critical issues of our time?

One of my basic assumptions is that the life journey of each of us is unique. We do not all share the same goals, in work or in any other area of life. Perhaps that is one of the factors that enables human society to function. There may be something ultimately meaningful and even holy in our diversity: that of God in everyone, different talents to contribute to some larger whole. I know that, as I encounter an incredible variety of qualities in my clients, I need always look for the distinctive frontier, that growing edge where the energies of each person are challenged and where they come alive.

Yet even as we journey in highly individual paths, we move

to some extent in concert. There is a basic rhythm in the process by which human beings grow. I have come to conceive it as a process of venturing and centering, an alteration of attending to our own issues as individuals, then reaching out to engage in the existence of others.

As we consider some specific ways to organize our working lives, it will be helpful to keep that cycle in mind. Sometimes, some of us will profit most from exploring what is going on or what ought to transpire out in the world—venturing. At other times, others of us will find it more important to "center down," addressing frontiers of the inner life. Both phases of the process are vital to our movement ahead in faith. Here, we begin with some approaches to clarifying the direction of our working lives— with the inward, centering side of the journey.

CHAPTER 4

CENTERING DOWN
The Process of
Self-Assessment

"Would you tell me, please, which way I ought to go from here?"

"That depends a good deal on where you want to get to," said the Cat.

Lewis Carroll

In every effort to find our way in the world of work, self-assessment is the place to begin, and for two reasons. The first has to do with the need for purposiveness and meaning.

Several years ago, some gerontologists surveyed attitudes of a group of retirement-age workers. The workers were asked to indicate, as they prepared for retirement, whether the sequence of jobs they had held fitted into any pattern for them, whether there was some meaning to the sequence; or whether, as Henry Ford once said of history, the jobs were simply "one damned thing after another." If a worker found some meaning in his job history, his was termed an "orderly career." If not, a "disorderly career." Two-thirds of the workers surveyed reported, at the end of their lives, that they had had disorderly careers!

Data such as these suggest the importance of clarifying direction in relation to work. For many people find themselves, throughout life, simply moving at random from one job to the next, finding no particular significance in the way they have spent about one-third of their lives. That process, at the time, may feel all right for some. But to the extent that integrity, or a sense of wholeness, is an important human concern—especially in old age—feeling that one has worked at random may give rise to a painful sense of futility (Erikson, p. 139).

We may find at the end of our working lives that we have met some social obligations, but not much more. In *Loon Lake* E. L. Doctorow's turn-of-the-century industrialist exhorts a young man to:

> Get in, get into the place that's your nature, whether it's running a corporation or picking daisies in a field, get in there and live to it, live to the fullness of it, become what you are, and I'll say to you, you've done more than most men. Most men . . . most of them don't ever do that. They'll work at a job and not know why. They'll marry a woman and not know why. They'll go to their graves and not know why.   (p. 110)

The second problem with failing to clarify direction is a bit less dramatic, but no less real. It is that apparent lack of focus detracts from our marketability. The most difficult type of client whom I try to help seek employment is the person who seems eager to do almost anything.

That condition keeps us in a passive role, dependent on the initiative of others. The anxiety of that role can obviate exploring and expressing ourselves. Chameleonlike, we may lose the capacity to present ourselves with any sort of distinctiveness, and come off rather gray. And so, we need to begin by clarifying our own direction.

The resources that follow can be helpful in that process. First, however, some words of caution are in order. While there are good benefits to be gained by communicating, as we are, through the pages of a book, there are some inherent limitations as well. You and I cannot engage in direct dialogue through this medium, and that is a particular disadvantage as I offer some exercises for self-assessment. In any process through which we take stock of ourselves, we need to find opportunities for dialogue, to avoid the "paralysis of analysis" that can accompany excessive introspection. It always is most beneficial to pursue self-assessment in partnership with some other person who both cares about you and has a good measure of objectivity. I can't be that kind of partner through these pages. So it may be helpful for you to jot down some of your responses to the issues I raise and to share them with a counselor or friend.

In addition, we ought to expect that your responses to these questions could change over time. If you write down some of your current thoughts, it may be helpful to review them in a few years.

We'll look now at several sets of issues: investment in work, life-work roles, career roles, and competencies. The symbol in Figure 3 may help us organize our impressions and ideas. What is that symbol? A set of lenses, perhaps, to be focused so as to clarify our vision. Or, a simple mandala—an Eastern, religious art form representing the balance of universal forces. For me the symbol suggests the importance of keeping multiple factors in view, while paying particular attention to the point where they cohere: the "stillpoint" as Taoists would say, where we might find a center. You may wish to color or shade or simply rank-order the spheres in each symbol, as a way of noting their present importance to you. We begin with levels of investment.

JOB, CAREER, VOCATION: LEVELS OF INVESTMENT IN WORK

The word "job" probably is derived from a Middle English term for "piece" or "lump." Career counselors think of a job as a piece of work that is prefabricated. An employer already has created the job; our task is to persuade him to give it to us. And a job

FIGURE 3

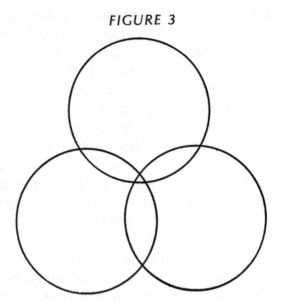

generally is held for secondary gain—pay, security, or the like—rather than for intrinsic value.

I overheard this conversation the other day in my supermarket:

Customer to the store guard, who has stood in the same spot for a half hour: "What's goin' on, Charlie?"

   Guard: "Oh, just trying to keep things on an even keel."
   Customer: "How do you like this work?"
   Guard: "What can I say? It's a living."

That's a job—working not for satisfaction, but for secondary gain. And, generally, working in a climate of insecurity—never certain of finding an employer to provide another job when we need one.

The literature on occupations in America, since World War II, has stressed "career planning" as an alternative to simply seeking and holding jobs. Many writers and counselors in private career consulting firms have pointed out the desirability of long-range planning in establishing a "career"—a sense of direction or progress through life. (The term career is derived from the Latin word for a two-rut track: *carraria*, literally "the way of the cart." The word "livelihood" has a similar origin as "life course.")

"Career management" has become a preoccupation for many professional workers in particular. By managing one's career, the theory goes, it is possible to transcend a process of shortsighted job seeking and to lay groundwork for a long-term progression through a series of positions that entail increasing levels of responsibility and income. The emphasis in this approach is on management in the sense of "control." Career management enables an individual to move beyond dependence on employers who reward job performance with extrinsic benefits such as salary and security. In a process of career management, while such factors continue to have importance, they are subordinate to self-direction. One knows why he is in a particular job, what he hopes to learn and gain, about how long he intends to stay there, and has some idea of the position he'd like to acquire as the next step in his career. In *Career Building*, Richard Germann writes:

> Good career planning will eliminate the need to act out of desperation. You will always know what your next step is and will have laid the groundwork to take it at any time. (p. 5)

Experience with hundreds of working adults has taught me the value of career management. Young adults in particular, a few years out of college, often need help in long-range planning. Many of them get mired in fortuitous first jobs that subsequently become meaningless.

> o Fred is typical. Following graduation from college as a math major with a good academic record, he took a job as a field engineer with a land surveying company. The position was a good one in many respects. Despite long hours, it was financially rewarding. And for a while it was interesting. Fred's math background enabled him to pick up the necessary skill quickly and to perform well. After a time, however, the work became boring. In a small firm, it didn't seem possible

to go anywhere; there was nothing else to learn. The job became simply part of Fred's daily routine. Finally, after five years with the survey company, Fred had had enough and came to see me. It wasn't long before we had reviewed his history on the job, compared that experience to his original interests as an undergraduate, and helped him relocate in a position as a statistical analyst with the home office of an insurance company. Fred's career now is back on track. He can see where he is going, both within the company and as a part-time graduate student in statistics. From "having a job," he has resumed a career.

o If the process of learning career management is important to young adults in dead-end jobs, it is even more critical for those in midlife. Sam is forty-five and has held fifteen jobs since college, in four different fields. For some people that kind of movement could represent progress, some kind of growth. But not for Sam. As we review his work history, it turns out that his personal life has been characterized by the same kind of fluidity. Sam has been married three times, under the auspices of three different religious denominations to which he has belonged. His career changes as well as the church memberships have been determined largely by the interests of his several wives. Sam has come to the realization that his career is more than "disorderly," it is running amok! At forty-five, he intends to learn some techniques of career management.

There is more, however, to the process of developing one's working life than career management. As important as it is to experience some sense of autonomy and career control, most people have deeper needs as well. Career control is, after all, a somewhat static concept, like "marital stability" or "mental health." Career management is an important precondition to fulfillment in one's working life, but not the full essence of it.

At a deeper level, most people want their working lives to

contribute to something of importance to them. Nora Watson, another of the workers interviewed by Studs Terkel, put it well:

> I think most of us are looking for a calling, not a job. Most of us, like the assembly line worker, have jobs that are too small for our spirit. Jobs are not big enough for people. (p. xxiv)

Nora's use of the word "calling" suggests an important theme in the human search for meaning—vocation.

The idea of vocation, in Biblical thought, derives from two terms. *Kalah* in Hebrew and *kaleo* in Greek both mean "to call," "to cry out," "to summon." The New Testament term that we translate "church," *ekklesia*, originally referred to a group brought together—summoned—by the cries of a herald. The thought carried over to the concept of vocation can be interpreted as "response." When we speak of an individual's vocation or calling, we give attention to whatever really counts in his world, that to which he responds ultimately.

> o The central event in Ed's life occurred during World War II when he was wounded in combat. Being a soldier had been the highlight of Ed's young life, and a source of great pride for his family. He was astonished by the realization that, in the midst of all the exhilaration of liberating France, someone actually had tried to kill him! That experience influenced him profoundly, and he kept a journal of his reactions during convalescence. Ed became a Quaker in the process of coming to terms with his wounds. He thought of developing a book from the journal. But as the war ended, other issues claimed his attention. Ed married and became the father of three children. He returned to school, using his GI Bill benefits to acquire a degree in urban planning.
>
> Ed did well enough as an urban planner. He rose to a position with the federal government where he earned a good salary and worked in a large office in Washington, DC. But the work was dismal—impersonal summaries of statistics in

which no one really took an interest. Still, he persisted in his career and saw his three kids through college.

He remembers the day he mailed his last check for tuition, for that was the day he resolved to quit. Ed now has a position in another field, and he spends his evenings at his typewriter—working on a manuscript titled "I've Been Wounded!"

o Susan's story began in young adulthood when she graduated from college as a psychology major and decided to pursue a master's degree in guidance and counseling. Her plans for a career in school counseling were set aside when she met Jim, and then married him. Jim was a talented young engineer, and their life together turned out to follow his rise, through several job transfers, in his profession. Between accompanying him, and raising two sons, there wasn't much room for Susan to pursue her own interests. She did work for a number of years as a college admissions counselor and at one point stayed with a school long enough to become an assistant dean of admissions. Due to Jim's success, Susan never found herself in financial need, so she didn't really have to work. But she always enjoyed her relationships with young people and their parents; that was her real reward.

When I met Susan as a student in one of my career development classes, she had been in Denver for several years. Jim had become a partner in a company here and, after finishing out the school year in Indiana, she had once again followed him at the cost of her own professional life. Susan was happy in Denver, but still a bit at loose ends. Should she once again seek employment as an admissions counselor? Age was becoming a problem; most of the admissions counselors were in their twenties. For another thing, she wasn't certain that was the way she wanted to invest her energies. Over the years, it had become apparent to her that many young people and their parents lacked an impartial source of good information about colleges. Selecting a college on the basis of talking with admissions counselors employed by the various schools was, after all, very much like buying a car or computer. You were sure to hear all the merits of the line sold by the sales representative you talked with, but very little about the competition. What seemed to be called for was a counseling/referral service through which young people and their parents could receive comprehensive, impartial guidance in college selection. Susan had acquired a wealth of information, materials, and contacts over the years. She was now sixty, and not getting younger. The time to try it seemed to be now!

And so, she did. After careful exploration of similar services in other parts of the country, interviews with several acquaintances who earned their living as consultants, inquiries about how to acquire a complete library of current catalogues, and a cost analysis of starting a business, she went ahead. Today the business is doing very well. Jim's sudden death two years ago left a void Susan still feels deeply. But the consulting practice is an important link with issues and relationships that span her life, and it provides a way of addressing a need that no one else had met.

Perhaps it's not coincidental that both these individuals who illustrate the theme of vocation are in advanced years. At that point in life, as Erik Erikson and others have suggested, issues of purpose and direction often are seen more clearly. And at that time financial independence may have been achieved. But similar questions and discoveries are potentially in the province of most people, from young adulthood onward.

Everyone has, at least in nascent form, some sense of what matters most to them, and of what it is they would like to contribute. Sometimes the sense of vocation derives from a particular area of expertise for which there seems to be a need, as with Susan. Sometimes it's an intrinsic gift or talent, such as the ancient Greeks conceived as *arete*. That term, usually translated "virtue," refers to a particular attribute or ability refined to the level of excellence. To think of an individual's "arete" is to bring into focus the specific skill that the person might wish to cultivate, often at the cost of subordinating every other part of his life.

Generally, people have an easier time finding focus if their abilities are somewhat circumscribed. The Johnson O'Connor Foundation, which offers aptitude testing services throughout the country, has found that "TMAs" (people with Too Many Aptitudes) frequently have lifelong difficulty settling on an occupation, since no work role enables them to use their full range of abilities.

There is a striking Zen Buddhist story of an individual discovering vocation in a limited sphere. A student of Zen lost his spiritual mentor. The student's efforts to pursue enlightenment under another teacher were entirely unsuccessful; he found that he remained too dependent on his deceased master for spiritual growth.

> Finally he came to the conclusion, "I am not destined in this life to attain understanding of reality, so it is best for me to devote myself to some meritorious work and wait for the next life for Enlightenment." So he thought he would take good care of a tomb where a famous Master was buried, and keep it clean to show his respect. One day he was cleaning the ground and happened to sweep a piece of stone which struck the root of a bamboo. This produced a certain sound. . . . (Suzuki, p. 79)

Something in the student resonated to that sound, and in the quiet depth of his response, suddenly a new and unimagined vista of enlightenment awakened within him. He had found his path. So it is that vocation sometimes may be found in simple tasks that claim our full attention.

Often, as in Ed's case, people discover direction in relation to some issue that they themselves have found especially challenging. Karen's interest in speech communication developed in the same way. Indeed, I've been struck by the number of professionals in the field of special education who themselves have suffered from physical handicaps or learning disabilities—how many of them, for example, wear hearing aids.

Other examples abound. I have an acquaintance whose recovery from surgery for a brain tumor left her with an impairment of short-term memory; she has taught courses in time management. The mother of another had a terrible experience in a nursing home, and Ginny became our state ombudsman for nursing home residents.

Richard Simmons, the impressario of fitness, developed his interest in weight loss when, as an obese three-hundred-pounder, he was hospitalized from the effects of a crash diet. Many of us seminary graduates who left school in the 1960s only to find ourselves out of touch with life in local churches or with fewer churches to serve, having struggled to market our own rather esoteric skills, have become career counselors.

So, very often, areas where we ourselves have struggled become focal points for vocation. (This is not to suggest, of course, that each of us should spend our lives working at problems we can't solve. It is possible to get too close to critical issues. I think of recovering alcoholics whose state of sobriety is so tenuous that they must spend all their time and energies rescuing others from drink. Or of a client I saw recently who entered a human-service profession not long after seeing her brother through a long, painful death from cancer. After a few years teaching handicapped children, she simply had to get away from the work; it was too close to the trauma of her brother's death.)

But, by and large, the approach is well-founded. To "come through" an experience such as these examples is to participate in a process of personal transformation. To find oneself motivated and free to help others across a past frontier is to become an agent of transformation in that process, and that may be the most personally enriching vocation of all.

What relationship can we find between our abilities and interests on the one hand, and our disabilities on the other? Many of us discover our life purpose, our sense of vocation, somewhere on the latter end of that continuum. The novelist John Fowles put it well: "We create out of what we lack, not what we have."

As you reflect upon the various levels of investment in occupation—job, career, vocation—you may want to note which of them best describes your present approach to paid employment, and which is farthest from the mark. (*See Figure 4.*) I suggest also that you note issues which may have the character of vocation for you—those about which, for whatever reason, you really care.

At this point, an uncomfortable question may arise. It's all well and good, we may feel, to think about the value of vocation as a sense of consequence in our work. But what about those of us who may not be able to serve our deepest commitments through paid employment? What's the relevance of "vocation" to us? How can we square what we must do for a living with what we really live to do?

I hear those questions from clients regularly, and know that they're not easy to resolve. My way of addressing them, again, is always to begin by trying to identify and clarify the sense of vocation. What are the particular needs that you or I would most like to address, the special gifts we hope to cultivate and share, the particular products or services we would like to provide? Once we have those issues to some degree in focus, we need to view them in the context of three larger, life roles:

WORKER, LEISURITE, VOLUNTEER*

Work, as we noted in the first chapter, is an integral part of life. Most of us meet many needs through our roles as workers, and it is important for most people to maintain involvement in the labor market. That is part of the challenge posed by "jobless growth." But working is not the totality of living. There may be important reasons to assess its place among other parts of our lives—not only in the interest of personal wholeness, but also to

---

*Donald Super, one of our leaders in the field of vocational guidance, has conceived the roles "worker, leisurite, and citizen." I prefer the term "volunteer" to "citizen," but find his schema very helpful in thinking about the ways we spend our lives.

FIGURE 4

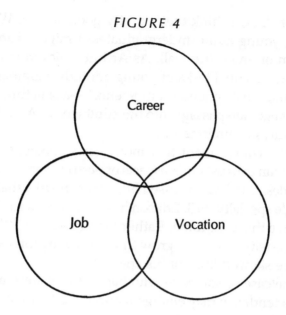

consider ways in which our vocational interests might be pursued outside paid employment.

I grew up in a business environment in which professional success meant a great deal. And I remember from my teenage years a conversation overheard by one of my father's employees. Fred was riding up in the elevator one morning as two workers lamented the death of another. "Such a shame!" said one. "He was so young!" the other responded. And then asked, too quickly, "Who's going to take his place?" That conversation helped Fred clarify his values, the amount of emphasis he chose to give his work. It confirmed my own intention to try to tackle larger issues of life, in the ministry.

The typical American middle-class male has been socialized to sandwich several decades of intense investment in work between segments of learning and leisure. During the past decade, females have drilled to the same cadence. The springboard to professional success, according to this scenario, is specialization. So, an elderly character in the film *Stay Hungry* advises his ne'er-do-well nephew, "To make anything of a life, it doesn't matter what you do. Just do something, and do it unsparingly!"

Some days, I think that's pretty good advice. Were I back teaching young adult undergraduates, I might even hang the quotation on my office wall. As Arthur Chickering has noted, one of the essential tasks of young adult development is to acquire some "instrumental competence"—a skill through which one can negotiate passage into the adult world. And developing skill requires commitment.

Yet the commitment that motivates someone to become a specialist can exhaust other aspects of personal life. Young adults, in their desire to build focused lives, may restrict their energies to a single specialty. Erik Erikson has coined the term "totalism" to describe this syndrome. Rather than exercising "the courage of his diversity," so as to grow full, the young totalist develops along the skewed lines of his specialty.

In the case of someone who has a strong *arete*, a particular gift, that tendency may emerge naturally. Other vocational motives, such as exposure to a great need, also may stimulate an individual to specialize so as to be of effective service.

But too often the need to throw all one's energies into work is fed by forces that vitiate the person. A French phrase, *professional deformation*, suggests the hazards of overinvestment in an occupational role. In that process, we can become deformed (Kolb, p. 183 and passim). A friend of mine never forgot a comment made in a management-training encounter group. One of his co-workers looked him in the eye and said, "You *are* your job!" I know people in sales who are their job; even after hours they can't stop trying to sell themselves to others. I know psychotherapists who can't put aside their guarded, professional manner to be spontaneous and relax with their friends.

Psychiatrists Jay Rohrlich (*Work and Love*) and Roger Gould (*Transformations*) have suggested that many of us become overinvested in adult work roles in the unconscious hope of leaving childhood insecurities behind. The workaholic is, at base, a frightened child.

o Or, in some instances, misinvested as an overly obedient child. Ted graduated from college with the dream of trying to become a novelist. He had experienced genuine intellectual excitement and worked to capacity for the first time during a senior-year semester in France. Ted had begun to come alive, and he started making plans to pursue his dream, following Hemingway's path around Europe, writing in outdoor cafés.

But as Ted talked over his plans with his parents, the dream began to fade. They never had been to college; his father had worked his way up from retail clerk to store manager through sheer determination. While Ted's parents wanted to be supportive of their son, they had made a financial sacrifice to help him through school. Roaming the Continent, trying to write a novel, seemed a frivolous use of his college degree.

Without ever being directed to do so, Ted relented and took a managerial-training position with a large department store. He worked hard and used his considerable talent to advantage. Within five years, Ted was assistant to the president. His ex-wife recalls his obsession with the retail business. Ted would discuss philosophies of trend merchandising with strangers at cocktail parties. At age forty, he achieved his goal in retailing and became owner of a small chain of stores.

And then, as he recalls, the flame went out. Ted lost interest in the store and in his marriage as well. "Everything went dark," he says. Ted began to drink, his depression deepened, and in the same year he lost his family and the stores.

Today there is a faint glow to his spirit and he is rebuilding his life. Still in his early forties, Ted knows that he has productive years ahead and he is beginning to explore several new opportunities. Each of them involves work he actually cares about. Ted has learned the cost of trying to build a life on someone else's dreams.

Specialization also may be motivated by the expectations of one's society. For advanced, technologically sophisticated societies depend on specialization. In *Two Essays on Analytical Psychology* Carl Jung observed:

> Society expects, and indeed must expect, every individual to play the part assigned to him as perfectly as possible, so that a man who is a parson . . . must at all times . . . play the role of parson in a flawless manner. Society demands this as a kind of surety: each must stand at his post, here a cobbler, there a poet. No man is expected to be both . . . because society is persuaded that only the cobbler who is not a poet can provide workmanlike shoes.   (p. 191)

It is important to remember that not all societies are specialized. I recall hearing of an anthropologist who visited an out-of-the-way tribe. The anthropologist was studying art in primitive cultures and he asked his native informants who their artisans were. The conversation stalled at the point of defining "art." "We have no word for that," the natives concluded. "But we all try to do everything the best we can!"

That approach to craft, in which everyone has some opportunity to create, seems to be characteristic of preindustrial societies. Gandhi tried hard to recover that spirit through restoration of a cottage industry in India. One of his associates, Ananda Coomaraswamy, saw deep into the basic human issues at stake. "It is not as if the artist were a special kind of man," he said. "Every man is a special kind of artist." For that reason, he believed, "The subdivision of labor is the assassination of a people."

The ancient Greek word *oikonomos*, from which we derive "economics," referred to the manager of a household. The householder developed every factor of productivity (see chapter 3) while specializing in none. To be a householder/generalist was to hold a respected position in the Hellenic world. In recent years, E. F. Schumacher in *Good Work* has written of the "homecomers" in Western society, and Alvin Toffler (*The Third Wave*) of the "prosumers," those who produce much of what they consume. Toffler cites impressive data to suggest that the numbers of do-it-yourself prosumers among us are growing significantly. Perhaps we are beginning to hear the counsel of Jung, Gandhi, Coomaraswamy, and others who, decades ago, were prophetic advocates of a balanced life.

One good way to pursue personal wholeness is to balance what we do for pay with voluntary service. My experience in and out of the ordained ministry has taught me a good deal about the role of volunteer. Fifteen years ago, when I left a position as college chaplain for a new career in adult education, I made some other significant life changes as well. One of these was becoming a Quaker. A feature of the Religious Society of Friends that attracted me was the traditional Quaker view that all of us followers and friends of Jesus are ministers together. As might be expected, that understanding of ministry radically diminishes the role of ordained clergy. Here I was with two advanced degrees from theological seminaries, and a Quaker! Nonetheless I appreciated the opportunity to participate in a fellowship of concern in which neither I nor anyone else was distinguished as clergy, a role in which I never had felt comfortable. Today I still find life as a Quaker enriching, and suspect that I have had a much more effective ministry in this tradition than when I was ordained.

But that life has not been without complications. One of them has been the question of earning a living. Fortunately, by the time I became a Quaker, I'd begun to establish my new career as an adult educator, translating my background in pastoral counseling into a new context.

Perhaps a more serious concern has been trying to serve my Friends Meeting (the counterpart to a local congregation), after working hours. I've learned, through hard experience, that those who would serve effectively in voluntary roles had best heed what they do for pay. The problem is not so much lack of time and energy to serve after hours as it is one of what particular energies remain. For, just as few significant writers have earned their living as professors of literature, since teaching demands the same creativity one calls upon to write, so it is with voluntary service.

I have found, for example, that the work I do in career counseling during the week precludes being much of a resource to those with personal problems within the Meeting. One year I served as convener of our pastoral care, Oversight Committee, and was less than effective. For, much as I cared for members of our Meeting and despite the fact that I possessed some counseling skills, at the end of a week's involvement with my clients' needs and problems, I dreaded even hearing of new ones.

On the other hand, I have found great satisfaction serving in areas unrelated to my paid employment, such as promoting a Third World economic development program sponsored by our Friends World Committee. Often, after devoting hours to that work, I've felt more energized than before, and have thought of Golda Meir's comment: "A new set of problems is as good as a vacation!"

Questions of logistics such as these are important because today some of our most vital opportunities for service are found in voluntary associations. Not only the conventional, sanctioned kind of social service agency such as the Red Cross or the Junior League, but genuinely innovative programs as well. Small independent associations of concerned citizens can be quietly effective catalysts of social change. Operation Crossroads Africa, which for years sponsored joint service projects for African and American college students, is but one example; it served as the model for John F. Kennedy's Peace Corps. (George Crowell's *Society Against Itself* offers a helpful, critical analysis of social service associations vis-à-vis social change.)

Voluntarism is one of our society's finest traditions, and for some of us the prime expression of vocation. But fulfilling important vocational concerns as a volunteer may entail significant tradeoffs in paid employment, for a job that demands little of one's energies—or those at least of a different kind.

The third role that can contribute to a balanced life is that of leisurite. As in the case of the role of volunteer, this role can be more than ballast. It is also a way of meeting important human needs.

Foremost among these needs may be letting go: Letting go of all the devices by which we try to mold the world. Letting go of all the care we invest in others' approval, performing on cue, providing what's expected. Letting go of every effort to reform the world, and opening up instead to all that is given and good in Creation.

I'm not proficient at this. My life easily gets out of balance, overinvested in work (especially when working to complete a book manuscript under deadline!) and in voluntary assignments. And so I turn now and again to some of my favorite passages of the *Tao*:

> As for those who would take the whole world
> To tinker as they see fit,
> I observe that they never succeed. . . .
>
> By letting go, it all gets done;
> The world is won by those who let it go!
> —(Blakney, pp. 81, 101)

There are places in our society where leisure has assumed high value, as was the case in Europe during the Renaissance, and in Hellenic Greece. Daniel Yankelovitch writes of management professionals in a plant in Tennessee who scrambled to apply for positions as custodians, presumably so that they could invest their energies in activities other than work. This attitude is especially pronounced in areas of high ambience. Management consultant Morris Massey cites the case of an employer in the Rockies who suspended some of his younger workers as punishment, but was shocked to find that they regarded fewer days work as more time for skiing and, thus, a reward. In *Nine Nations of North America* Joel Garreau has commented that in the Eastern, heavy industrial region he calls The Foundry, working seems to be the only reason people live there. I have wondered how Harvey Brenner's study of morbidity and mortality related to unemployment would compare to the experience of residents of San Diego or Tampa!

Perhaps, as a race, our ultimate response to jobless growth will be to value leisure more. In the process we may discover another fulfilling use of free time—that leisure can be time for learning.

LEARNING AS ADULTS

In the late 1960s, Allen Tough launched an innovative program of research into the learning lives of adults. Tough, who at the time was a doctoral student at the University of Chicago, was interested in the relationship of *learning* (i.e., "highly deliberate efforts to gain and retain some definite knowledge or skill") to other forms of growth during adulthood. He sensed that the learning activities of adults extended considerably beyond formal education, and coined the term "learning projects" to identify them.

Tough defined a learning project by simple standards. It was to be an effort that involved at least seven hours' activity, in periods of at least one hour, in which an individual's primary intention was to learn. Using some basic survey techniques, Tough began to interview adult Chicagoans of many ethnic backgrounds and ages about their lives as learners. His first subjects were drawn from a variety of occupational groups and included elementary school teachers, factory workers, and lawyers.

In subsequent years, Tough (who now is an adult educator and researcher in Toronto) and others have repeated the original survey many times, in other areas of the United States as well as in Canada, Ghana, Jamaica, and New Zealand. The results, as Tough summarizes them, have challenged some traditional assumptions about learning:

> Despite the diversity of regions and populations studied, a remarkably consistent pattern of lifelong learning emerged. One surprising facet of this picture is the amount of learning. About 90 percent of all adults conduct at least one major learning effort each year. The average person conducts five distinct learning projects in one year—that is, in five distinct areas of knowledge, skill, or personal change. The person spends an average of 100 hours per learning effort in a year, which adds

up to a total investment of 500 hours in all of his or her efforts in the year. That is almost 10 hours a week, on the average—a lot of time!   (Chickering, p. 297)

As one might expect, the subjects studied by Tough's adult learners were diverse. Much of the study had to do with work—preparing for one's chosen occupation, preparing for a change in career, or simply learning what is needed to perform one's job. (Attorneys, for example, were continuously engaged in learning as they prepared for upcoming cases.) Other learning related to managing the home or family. Often, adults engage in research of a product before buying it. Some learning related to circumstances of life as a single adult—managing social relationships, for example, or finances.

Others approached finances even more seriously, studying the stock market through investigating particular industries or the economy in general. Some found their interest invested in political or other social issues; parents, for example, might seek to become better informed about their children's schools.

A good deal of adult learning related to some hobby, such as learning a second language, or to a craft such as woodworking, or playing a musical instrument. (More than one American in five plays an instrument.) Other learning involved exploration of religious or philosophical issues, from the fundamental growth-questions of childhood: Who am I? Who are you? and What is the world like?

It is interesting, also, to observe some of the characteristic ways in which adults learn. Research has shown that adult learners have a strong interest in the application of new knowledge. Most of their learning is problem- or task-centered. Only about 10 percent of adult learning projects were pursued in classes, and only 5 percent were motivated by academic credit. Indeed, only one project in five was planned by a professional. In addition to the 75 percent that were planned by the learner himself or herself, another 3 or 4 percent received assistance—from a friend, or a group of peers.

Adult learning is basic to the process of keeping oneself alive and growing in a constantly changing world. It thrives on forces that infuse personal growth in general, such as curiosity, wonder, and the wish to become free. Learning, essentially, is an enjoyable activity; young children love to learn. Yet many adults have found the process stifled by schools. That may be one reason why so much of adults' learning is self-directed. All adults know that the time of life is finite. That may be the reason adults give attention to the concrete application of their learning—why the tone of even their most abstract learning projects remains pragmatic, addressing an immediate problem to be resolved.

Allen Tough's exploration of learning highlights a deep level of adult life which traditionally we have undervalued or ignored. He comments:

> People seem eager to talk about their learning efforts, partly because they rarely have a chance to describe them in detail to an interested listener. Although trying to improve oneself—to gain new knowledge or become a better person in some way—is certainly an exciting part of one's life, people do not usually discuss their learning adventures and process at parties or the dinner table. (p. 297)

Perhaps we should become more appreciative of what we're learning and more open to share it. Tough's studies suggest that there's quite a lot of learning going on!

Here is a commentary by a fifty-one-year-old student:

> Last spring I made a commitment to myself. Several times in the past 25 years I had started to continue my education, but it seemed that always there was one thing or another that would prevent me from finishing. Indeed, I would only get started in most cases and then a change in job responsibilities, a physical move, a baby born or some other important life event would jump up to interrupt my education. But last spring I definitely decided to return to college and earn a degree in accounting, regardless of the circumstances. . . .
>
> During the period after I had talked with our personnel

man [about possible college programs] and the time that I investigated the University Without Walls program, I developed a very strong desire to learn all that I possibly could about everything. Although my plan for achieving a degree did not change, I clearly changed my emphasis from a "degree" to "learning" without any time limits. . . .

In the beginning the goal of achieving a college degree was important to me only for peer-acceptance reasons. As time passed this concern had become less critical to me because of my ability to keep up with my work responsibilities. Therefore, each time that my education was interrupted I was in no hurry to re-enter the educational process. When I finally came to the realization that the value of education was in giving me growth and not for peer-impression, my educational goals took on real meaning.

My life and outlook have changed considerably, as my craving for knowledge has intensified. I believe this to be a bedrock decision and a lifelong search.

It may be that learning is only one of many leisure activities we underrate, and that you and I could benefit from considering regularly areas in which we're living as leisurites, or serving as volunteers, as well as the responsibilities we fulfill as workers. In Figure 5, we find our symbol again. Jot down some notes on important activities in each sphere of your life, and rank order the sectors.

Finally, let's reflect upon our life-work relationship to three career roles, and to the broad issue of competence.

CAREER ROLES

The novice, the expert, the mentor—these are the three essential roles in every person's working life. Essential roles, but often unrecognized. Understanding them can help clear up much of the confusion many of us find in our careers.

To a degree, each of the three roles—novice, expert, mentor—characterizes a different phase of life. The young adult is a novice,

FIGURE 5

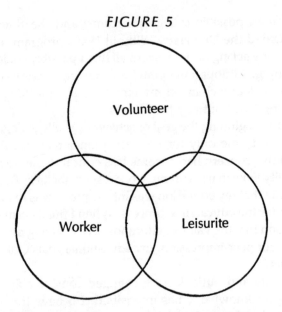

new to the responsible roles and skills of adulthood. The central task for young adults is, to use Daniel Levinson's phrase, "getting into the adult world."

This process apparently is becoming more complex and taking longer than it used to. It is not uncommon today to meet thirty-year-olds who have yet to take on personal or professional roles of adulthood. Whether because of violent encounters with figures of authority during the late 1960s or empathy for their parents' marital and job frustrations—for whatever reasons, many people in our society are living longer in the role of novice:

> ◦ Ken looked young when I first knew him, perhaps twenty-five. In fact he was over thirty, and that was part of his problem. Over thirty, and still stuck in a dead-end job, finishing floors. Twelve years before, in college, he'd had dreams of being an architect. However, in the middle of his junior year he encountered two tough courses, and his grades began to slide. That led to the loss of his scholastic deferment and a year-long process of appeals to his draft board. During this time, he brooded about the war he might be drafted into, and his grades got steadily worse. Ultimately, feeling completely

powerless, he was sent to Vietnam; he served there two years.

Ken came home and tried to resume his studies, but his sense of purpose and direction was gone. Something about the experience of growing up under the shadow of the draft haunted him, left him feeling as powerless as before. So he dropped out—and not just from school. For almost ten years, Ken drifted in and out of jobs and relationships, avoiding any serious involvement with the adult world. Facing the prospect of losing his job, he made an important decision: to try again to make some serious advancement in his career. It isn't easy—getting into the adult world at thirty!

Eventually, often with the help of more experienced persons who care about our progress, most of us trade the role of novice for that of expert. Becoming more or less adept, we master some skill or body of knowledge and we find a place in the adult world. The role of expert permeates midlife.

Women, if they've had a family early, on the traditional schedule, have mastered the domestic scene by this time, though they may feel off-stride, still a novice, in the labor market. Coming out of the home, they may encounter only entry-level jobs at a time when their husbands and other male peers are at the height of their influence. Other women, those who have put careers first, may experience a painful void in their personal lives.

While some men may glory in their expertise and status, the wish to let the other half live, to de-emphasize one's career, is widespread as well. In midlife, the age of expertise, it is difficult for individuals, let alone couples, to balance their personal and professional needs.

i have noticed
that men
somewhere around forty
tend to come in from the field
with a sigh
and removing their coat in the hall
call into the kitchen

you were right
grace
it ain't out there
just like you've always said
    and she
    with the children gone at last
    breathless
    puts her hat on her head
the hell it ain't
    coming and going
    they pass
    in the doorway
                    Ric Masten,
        "Coming and Going," p. 14

And then one day the role of expert turns into something else, since no one can stay in the saddle forever. Ideally there is the role of mentor, ready and waiting, as the expert retires from active service.

> o The guest on Dick Cavett's show is unusually diffident, and Cavett is hard put to get him talking. A distinguished retired advertising executive in his midseventies, the guest has been responsible for many creative innovations in outdoor advertising, such as billboards that blew smoke rings and others with waterfalls. Photographs of these landmark advertisements are shown. The guest, still ill at ease, reminisces about his career, he and Cavett laughing nervously at forced jokes about the past. It looks like a long half hour.
>
> Then, midway through the show, the guest suddenly comes alive. There has been some mention of his adjustment to retirement. In fact, he says, rather than retiring he has recently started a whole new career, utilizing the technology from his fancy outdoor advertisements in proposals to illuminate some of the beautiful buildings of his home, New York City. He describes some of his proposed projects, the buildings and their histories, the lighting problems involved, and

his own new role as an advisor on architecture and lighting to public officials.

No, he hasn't retired—and that's why he isn't very good at reminiscing! He's found a way to translate the skills of a lifetime into a creative but manageable new venture. He is alive and growing, a prime example of the mentor reworking his career.

Ideally, there is a quiet and honored place from which to offer counsel to the next generation coming down the line. A few fields regularly offer this opportunity. Retired/fired coaches offer analytic comments on football telecasts. "Furloughed" pilots give flying lessons.

But more often, in a complex society caught up in rapid technological change, there is no such chance. Life moves so fast these days that it's hard to remain informed, much less expert, in one's field. Very often there is no place for the sage.

There are times when society behaves as though it wishes there were more roles for aging mentors. Thus we seem to flirt with Richard Nixon: "What's your view of . . . ?" The former President responds in a much-publicized series of interviews with a newspaper columnist, and in another series with a television-news commentator. But then, when he suggests that he might offer advice on foreign affairs to the new administration, there is a great public outcry of revulsion. Nixon is reassigned the role of retiree-in-disgrace. Is our reaction simply a further rejection of Richard Nixon the individual? Or is there indeed no place for the sage in our society?

The problem of finding mentor roles for older adults suggests another way of thinking about novices, experts, and mentors. (*See Figure 6.*) Perhaps these roles aren't necessarily age-bound at all. Perhaps we ought to consider the possibility of alternating these roles throughout the entire course of life.

The image of a career as a cycle suggests that we give thought to the areas of life in which each of us is functioning as novice, expert, or mentor at any given time. (*See Figure 7.*) The spheres

FIGURE 6

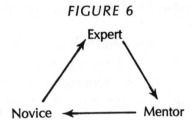

of our symbol offer an opportunity to note your relationship to these roles. What are your important current activities in each area, and what is the relative importance of the roles to you? As you view your life five years from now, do you foresee significant changes?

The cyclical career model suggests some creative possibilities in orchestrating these roles. For example, as marriage partners or friends or parents, we might pay attention to differences in roles and the rhythm of career development between ourselves, and look for ways to help one another manage that process. A husband might try to understand and support his wife in her role as novice in a new job; a teenager might be helped to master a skill or two, using the skills not only for income but also to offset the uncomfortable dependency of a long novitiate in school; and an older adult might be assisted in translating the skills and knowledge of a lifetime into a useful mentor role.

Today, finding appropriate mentoring and other work roles for older adults is an important concern of individuals who are not ready to retire on schedule. Some of these "new elders" seek work in order to generate income as they cope with an uncertain economy. Others, in the absence of clearly defined roles for older members of our society, continue employment so as to maintain involvement in their communities through their work roles (Kouri, "The New Elders").

In some professions, people may not mature till elder years. The Canadian adult educator, John McLeish, has summarized studies on creativity in various arts and academic fields. In *The Ulyssean Adult* he reports that some of the most productive

FIGURE 7

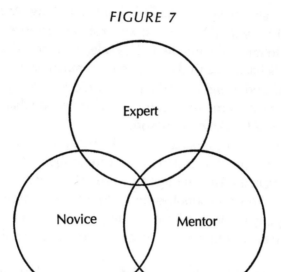

years for many people in the areas of the humanities, for example, are the seventh and eighth decades of life.

Still others may not find clear vocational focus until the years we have come to associate with retirement. Important voluntary roles, for example, may not crystallize till later years.

> o Jim Corbett grew up as the son of a lawyer in the ranch-lands of central Wyoming. In the summers, he worked on ranches. But he was a bright student who loved to read, and so he left Wyoming to earn bachelor's and master's degrees in philosophy. He was admitted to a doctoral program in philosophy, but found at that point in young adulthood that there were no philosophical issues about which he cared enough to invest several more years in graduate school. He did feel an interest in helping others to organize their scholarly pursuits, and so he completed a master's degree in library science.
>
> Jim never felt at home as a librarian. There was something of the Socratic gadfly in him, and he always found himself asking hard questions of his colleges' administrators—always

in hot water, never lasting in one job very long. At length, he and his wife decided that his best career move was to return to ranching and the independence it afforded; cattle can't talk back! The Corbetts settled into ranching in southern Arizona and found a good life. They did feel in need of an intellectually stimulating community, and found that among a group of Quakers in Tucson.

The dramatic change in their lives happened almost by accident, when Jim and his wife were in their late fifties. A Friend from the Tucson Meeting asked to borrow the Corbetts' van to take some supplies down to a Quaker project in a nearby city in Mexico. That evening, hours after the van was to have been returned, Jim became worried and called the police.

He found his friend and the van at a US border patrol station south of Tucson. It seemed that a hitchhiker whom the friend had picked up a few miles north of the border turned out to be a political refugee from El Salvador; both men were being held in custody. In the course of negotiating his friend's release, Jim learned a great deal about the circumstances of the Salvadoran refugee. The part of Jim that always had cared for truth and justice was triggered, and at a deep level. For unlike the trivial tempest-in-a-teapot of college politics, these issues were momentous. People were fleeing for their lives, from circumstances closely related to the foreign policy of the United States. As he watched the refugee deported to face the hazards he had fled, Jim knew he had found himself in a place from which he could not in conscience walk away. Today he is on trial as one of our national leaders in the ecumenical Sanctuary movement, representing needs of political refugees throughout Central America.

While today what people do in later life is largely a personal matter, manifested in a fascinating variety of forms, in the future that will change. The employment of older workers will become an important economic issue for our entire society. For one thing, dramatic demographic changes are beginning to have a significant impact on our economy. Currently the over-age-sixty-five segment of our population is growing at a rate twice that of the general populace. Under present trends, by the year 2000 the population of the United States will have increased three times during the century. But the number of those over age sixty-five will have increased ten times! During the 1970s the death rate among persons older than sixty-five fell 14 percent. (Elliot Brower of the US Department of Labor notes that, whereas in the case of infant mortality medical science in the United States probably has achieved all the gains that we can expect, when it comes to prolonging life this is not true. Longevity has not yet "topped out.") Life expectancy in the United States has increased by more than twenty-five years since 1900. By the year 2000 there will be about as many Americans over sixty-five as under twenty-one.

At the same time, our birth rate has been declining. The number of new births in the United States now stands below the "replacement rate." Teenagers already are outnumbered by those over age sixty-five. A related factor has to do with the timing of retirement. Whereas "retirement" is a relatively recent social institution, virtually unknown before this century, its popularity (if not its social viability) has grown. From 1950 to the mid-1970s, labor-force participation by workers over sixty-five declined by 50 percent for men, and by 10 percent for women. In the fifty-five to sixty-four-year-old age group (commonly referred to by gerontologists as the "young old") between 1970 and 1980 the rate of workforce participation by males declined from 83 percent to 72 percent. In the case of men over age sixty-five, the change is even more dramatic. As late as 1950, 41 percent of men over sixty-five were still in the workforce; in 1960 that figure dropped to 31 percent; in 1970 only 25 percent were still employed.

The tendency for older workers, living longer, to retire earlier, is related to several factors. One explanation for early retirement is that the educational level of present retirement-age persons is relatively low. Workers age sixty-five and over who are out of the labor force have a median education level of ninth grade. Only 15 percent have attended college. Comparative data show that it is persons who have little education, who serve in un-skilled, hourly wage jobs, who are the first to retire. By contrast, the "baby-boom" cohort—those 76-million Americans who were born between 1946 and 1964, and who by 1990 will constitute one-third of the population in this country—were educated at a time when college enrollments increased threefold. They are a highly trained segment of the workforce that has been eager to find creative, well-paid employment. They are likely to want to remain employed far longer than have their parents.

The other factor relating to current high levels of early re-tirement also relates to the "baby-boomers." In the interest of accommodating these many entrants to the workforce, American employers often have been forced to crowd out otherwise valued older employees.

> o Al is an example, forcibly retired from the aircraft manu-facturer for whom he had worked for twenty-five years. Al had fallen victim to demographic changes in America, for as the numbers of young adults declined, military recruiters found themselves hard-pressed to fill their quotas of volun-teers. In an attempt to "sweeten the pie," the military decided to turn to contractors, such as Al's firm, to create additional training opportunities for their volunteers. Al one day was introduced to a new "retirement counselor" from the per-sonnel department. In spite of the fact that he enjoyed his job, had a fine work record, and was in excellent health at age sixty-two, Al was induced to retire from his position as director of purchasing. There was a big party, and Al went home to try to fill his time with hobbies.

At present, with members of the baby-boom cohort still push-ing into the labor force, the question of employing older workers remains on our society's back burner. But already the issue is beginning to surface, the tip of what will become a very large iceberg: the problem of funding retirement pension programs. Again a few statistics can outline the situation. When Social Security was established in 1935, life expectancy was sixty-one years; the average person was not expected to live long enough to collect benefits. Life expectancy now has reached the mid-seventies and, as I've noted, is still rising.

When pension plans, augmenting Social Security, were implemented after World War II, the ratio of workers to retirees was about twenty to one. In 1970 that figure was eight to one. Now the ratio is six to one, and by the year 2000 it is likely to approach three to one. James Jorgenson, in his book *The Graying of America*, predicts that by the year 2035 the number of Americans reaching age sixty-five may have increased by more than 120 percent without a concomitant increase in the number of younger workers to pay benefits.

At about the year 2010, when the baby-boom generation arrives at what we now conceive as retirement age and the dependency ratio approaches three employed workers for every retiree, pension arrangements of the present finally will come asunder. By then, under current policies, expenditures for aging programs will consume 40 percent of the federal budget.

Today our society continues to confront the need to provide more jobs for the baby-boom cohort and, thus, finds it expedient to ease older workers such as Al out of the workforce. But the handwriting is on the wall. Eventually we will have to re-examine our assumptions about work in relation to age and, in the words of gerontologist Bernice Neugarten, reset the social clock. As a consequence, the institution of retirement as we know it is unlikely to outlast this century. Eventually the enterprise of helping individuals to reorganize their working lives in later years, rather than abandon them, will turn out to be in our national interest. Then we will find significance in the notion of "third career" planning—developing strategies for enabling individuals to build upon the "first career" of education and the "second career" of full-time employment to construct a scaled-down style of working in later years, a third career.

o The influence of economic and demographic changes on work roles came home the other morning at breakfast. One of our neighbors, a single woman, had awakened twice in the past few months to find an intruder in her house. One terrifying morning, she'd found the man behind her with a knife in bed. Kay had managed to talk him out of raping her, and he'd left by whatever way he'd come, but the assault to her psyche was real.

"Did you hear who broke into Kay's place?" one of the kids asked. "It was the paperboy!"

The paperboy? Images of twelve-year-old rapists, on bicycles, in braces. . . . But then we stopped to consider who delivers the newspaper these days. Sure enough, with scarce jobs and a growing shortage of teenagers, we are beginning to see more and more ads enticing adults to take on paper routes, and more adults making a full-time job of covering multiple routes. Kay's assailant was the "paperboy." Talk about resetting the social clock!

THE QUESTION OF COMPETENCE

Thus far, we have looked at issues affecting personal direction from several subjective points of view, which are related to lifestyles, stages, and values. In the next section, we'll explore some strategies for venturing out into the marketplace. Before moving to that phase, though, we need to address a final assessment issue: competence. Realistically, what is the relationship of our abilities and skills to what we might hope to accomplish?

When it comes to assessing competence, most of us have learned to rely on the expertise of specialists such as industrial psychologists. And there are occasions, as when selecting qualified candidates for a rigorous degree program, or choosing someone for a job that requires certain skills, when specialists in assessment may be needed.

Yet there are good reasons for more of us to become more self-reliant in understanding and evaluating our abilities. For one thing, many methods commonly used to identify work-related skills have come under serious criticism, and even been objects of litigation in recent years. The accustomed practice of employers to require certain academic credentials arbitrarily was challenged in the Supreme Court's *Griggs v. Duke Power* decision, in which an applicant for a custodial job protested the employer's requirement of a high-school diploma. That challenge was successful, and subsequent legal decisions have supported the view that selection of employees must be based on accurate assessment of skills directly related to requirements of a job (Kolb, p. 7).

It is clear that we need sound instruments to assess individual competence for specialized functions. But in general, I believe we need a broader view of competence as well, less dependent on those who specialize in assessment. In my work I find that most of us who are seeking new direction have a pretty good idea about the quality of what we've done in the past. We are, potentially, our own best authorities on what we do well and what we don't. We need to understand our own patterns of aptitude.

I have found David Kolb's Competency Circle especially helpful in that process. Kolb is a social psychologist who heads the Department of Organizational Behavior in the Weatherhead School of Management at Case Western Reserve University. His particular interest over the years has been in understanding competency in relation to other important attributes of a person such as learning style. In his book *Experiential Learning* Kolb describes how his own interest in this subject developed. As is so often the case, it originated with an unsolved problem.

> Several years ago, I served as a freshman advisor to undergraduates in a technological university. Two or three of my students in each group faced the awkward realization near the end of their freshman year that a career in engineering was not quite what they had imagined it to be. What to do? Transfer to a liberal arts school and possibly lose the prestige of a technological education? Endure the institute's technological requirements and "bootleg" a humanities major? Switch to management? Most decided to wait and see, but with a distinct loss of energy and increase in confusion. I felt powerless about what to advise or even how to advise. . . .
>
> It was only later that I was to discover that these shifts represented something more fundamental than changing in-

terests—that they stemmed in many cases from fundamental mismatches between personal learning styles and the learning demands of different disciplines.   (p. 163)

Kolb began to develop an instrument to assess learning styles, and found that individuals in different academic disciplines and professional roles differed in the ways they preferred to learn. By helping people outside these fields compare their needs and preferences as learners to those already practicing there, he was able to assist them in making more informed decisions about college majors or occupations that might fit. (That instrument, the *Learning Style Inventory*, is available from McBer and Company of Boston.) Kolb's subsequent work has focused on competencies related to the learning styles. I have broadly summarized the results of his research in both areas in Figure 8, replacing some of his technical terms with labels of my own:

The Competency Circle represents four basic modes of activity related to work: *influencing* others, *responding* to others, *analyzing* ideas or data, and *producing* tangible outcomes through mechanical or clerical tasks. These categories provide a way of understanding individual competencies and learning styles—i.e., the kinds of skills we now possess, and those that we are likely to want to develop.

This pie chart represents an idealized, perfectly symmetrical pattern of competencies, such as we might expect to find in the general population. Some workers, according to this model, could be expected to function primarily through *influencing* other people (as in sales, or management roles). Some would prefer to work with others in the context of *responding* to their needs (as in counseling or customer service). Some would be invested in *analyzing* systems of ideas or data (as, for example, in creating automated accounting systems or researching credit laws). And some would prefer to turn out tangible products—to "think with their hands" as one mechanic expressed it; in addition to mechanical tasks, clerical activities would be found in this *producing* sector as well.

The most subtle distinction in this chart, yet often the most

FIGURE 8

COMPETENCY CIRCLE

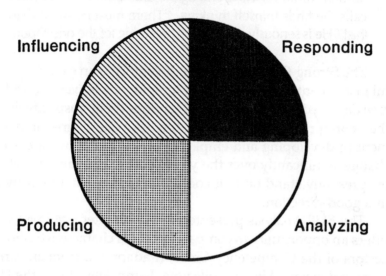

Influencing · Responding · Producing · Analyzing

critical, involves *influencing* and *responding*. To the degree that any of us is a "people person," and desires to work with others, it is important to understand in which of these ways we wish to function.

> o Recently, in the same day, I met with two people in their midtwenties. Linda had been employed for three years in a human service agency. With cutbacks in funds, her halfway house had been directed to admit violence-prone clients for whom it lacked adequate facilities. One of her friends on the staff had been badly beaten, and now every day at work Linda felt afraid. But, in addition, she was simply tired of attending to needy people. She wanted a more active, persuasive role through which to work with others, and some more visible reward. She thought of a career in sales.

> o Ray has been in sales for three years, and has done well selling office furniture. Last year, at age twenty-six, he made almost $40,000 and won a district award from his company. But he is a deeply caring individual, and he finds his work

Centering Down • **89**

lacking in depth. Whatever the personal complexity and needs of his customers, Ray's professional role is restricted to their furniture. Time and again, after a long day of sales calls, he finds himself thinking, "There must be more than this!" He is seriously considering preparing for the priesthood.

The Strong-Campbell Interest Inventory is an especially useful instrument for evaluating an individual's *influencing* and *responding* needs. (The Inventory identifies them, respectively, as the "enterprising" and "social" themes.) Our degree of investment in developing and employing skills in the two areas can change significantly over the years, and understanding where we presently stand on that continuum can be vital to growing in a good direction.

The Skill Analysis presented in this chapter (*see Exercise 1*), offers an opportunity to compare personal characteristics to the sectors of the Competency Circle. (I adapted it from an earlier version developed by my colleague, Joann Albright, of the University of Denver.) You may wish to complete the exercise and the others that follow, as you read along. In workshops, I ask people to compare the amount of marking they have done in the columns. Those that are heavily checked and underlined probably represent areas in which the individual has some significant investment and demonstrated ability. I then ask them to label the columns according to the Competency Circle. Column I represents the *Influencing* sector; II, *Responding*; III, *Analyzing*; and IV, *Producing*.

Sometimes, in addition, it is helpful for us to engage in a kind of "decomposition analysis," sifting among various components of past jobs. The Task/Skill Analysis (*see Exercise 2*), is useful for that purpose.

Materials of this kind can help us separate the wheat of our experience from the chaff. Often I help people do this by asking them to use a yellow felt pen (with markings one can see through) to cross through skills and specialized knowledge that they possess but don't wish to use. All of us have nonmotivated skills, and it's important to isolate them. Then I ask them to mark with a bright red felt pen any item in their analysis which might represent a growing edge—an area where they may have little skill but potential interest as a novice.

Motivated skills (those we wish to use) can be summarized as "capabilities" or "qualifications" in a functional/chronological résumé, as in the following examples. Sometimes it is helpful to write a preliminary summary of our skills by quadrant—for example what are the analytical skills that appear in my task/skill analysis?

Self-assessment methods of the kind described above can be particularly valuable in a changing society such as ours. And most of us can learn them, though sometimes we'll require help from a thoughtful counselor or friend. The people who require a full battery of aptitude testing are those whose experience is very limited because of age or from having spent years in a restricted occupational role such as airline pilot or housewife. In addition I occasionally meet the "TMA"—Too Many Aptitudes—person to whom I referred above. In any of these instances, I recommend a good aptitude-testing program such as that of the Johnson O'Connor Foundation (see Appendix) or, where that is not available or affordable, the General Aptitude Test Battery—GATB—which is administered through most community colleges and vocational schools. They usually offer the Strong-Campbell Interest Inventory as well.

But, generally, most of us can benefit from identifying and reflecting carefully upon the component parts of our work and other significant experiences—highlighting those in which we did something well, enjoyed doing it, and feel good about having done it. We can expect to find areas of ability and others of disability. Our expertise, generally, will appear in the former, and we'll do well to take note of foundations on which we might build higher skills.

It may be equally important, however, to give attention to sectors of the Competency Circle in which we're underdeveloped. Kolb's research suggests that as we mature we develop a greater need and capacity for integrating skills in our weaker areas with those in which we're strong. We become better able

EXERCISE 1

SKILL ANALYSIS

1. Read the list of skills below and check those which express something you can do.
2. Place a second check beside those verbs which express something you do well.
3. Circle those skills you especially enjoy using.

I. _____	II. _____	III. _____	IV. _____
administering ____	asking ____	assessing ____	assembling ____
advocating ____	assisting ____	clarifying ____	building ____
addressing ____	caring ____	classifying ____	cataloging ____
assigning ____	collaborating ____	defining ____	compiling ____
bargaining ____	communicating ____	detailing ____	computing ____
coordinating ____	contributing ____	detecting ____	constructing ____
delegating ____	counseling ____	diagnosing ____	designing ____
enlisting ____	consulting ____	editing ____	drawing ____
evaluating ____	encouraging ____	examining ____	gathering ____

expediting ———
facilitating ———
implementing ———
initiating ———
inspiring ———
leading ———
managing ———
marketing ———
motivating ———
negotiating ———
organizing ———
persuading ———
publicizing ———
selling ———
supervising ———
team-building ———

entertaining ———
explaining ———
guiding ———
helping ———
identifying ———
interpreting ———
listening ———
perceiving ———
reacting ———
recommending ———
reconciling ———
sensing ———
serving ———
supporting ———
trouble-shooting ———
understanding ———

investigating ———
judging ———
memorizing ———
modifying ———
organizing ———
reading ———
reasoning ———
reporting ———
researching ———
reviewing ———
solving ———
studying ———
summarizing ———
systematizing ———
thinking ———
visualizing ———

graphing ———
grouping ———
maintaining ———
making ———
mapping ———
operating ———
processing ———
programming ———
recording ———
renovating ———
repairing ———
reproducing ———
scanning ———
shaping ———
tabulating ———
updating ———

EXERCISE 2

TASK/SKILL ANALYSIS

Please note tasks that you perform during a typical day—either at work or in a significant voluntary role—and the skills that are necessary to perform these tasks. Indicate any special equipment or specialized knowledge necessary to perform these tasks. (In the context of this analysis, a "task" can be thought of as anything one does in the course of a working day. A skill is an ability that enables one to perform the task. Specialized knowledge or equipment are resources that may be required to use the skill. For example, an accountant prepares a tax-return TASK, using SKILLS in the areas of tax law and accounting principles and, perhaps, some SPECIALIZED KNOWLEDGE of regulations that apply to the client's industry as well as SPECIALIZED EQUIPMENT such as a particular type of computer and software program.)

Don't be concerned about adhering strictly to these categories; it is not essential that TASKS and SKILLS be distinguished with absolute consistency. The purpose of this analysis is to identify the component parts of a job, so that they can be seen in relation to other kinds of activity.

Also, describe briefly any personal qualities that would be beneficial in performing the tasks you have listed (such as orientation to detail, or ability to manage stress). Finally, think about the standards by which success in your tasks can be measured and note any ideas that come to mind under "success criteria." Frequently conflicts between employees and employers arise from their differing definitions of "success." (A commercial artist reports, for example, that his clients must evaluate the work he undertakes by the criteria "quality," "cost," and "time of production." They can have any two of these, he says, but not all three!)

(Example)

The following is an analysis of a summer job I held as an admissions counselor for Yankton College in South Dakota in the summer of 1958.

Tasks

Set appointments with prospective students. Interviewed prospective students and their parents to determine educational interests and needs. Gave talks about the college to church youth groups.

Skills

Ability to organize and schedule recruiting trips. Knowledge of the college's curriculum in relation to various courses of study. Public speaking.

Specialized Knowledge/Equipment

Offered insights based on my own experiences as a student at the college. Developed a slide presentation and printed handout materials for the talks.

Personal Qualities

Enthusiasm for the college. Honesty in acknowledging the limits of my knowledge, and of the college's resources in certain areas.

Success Criteria

For me: the accuracy with which I transmitted information. For the college: the number of students I recruited.

Tasks: The sequence of steps which were required to perform the stated task.
Skills: The ability required to perform the task.
Specialized Equipment/Knowledge: Technology and/or specialized knowledge required to perform the task.

Tasks	Skills	Equipment/Knowledge	Personal Qualities	Success Criteria

RITA

Address

Phone

Objective A position utilizing skills in public relations, marketing and financial analysis.

Qualifications *Public Relations*
Experienced in design and development of a comprehensive corporate public relations program.
Includes identification of various segments (media,
individual investors, industry, regulatory, investment
professionals) and determining appropriate media
vehicles for each public. Implementation and
follow-up of program.
Produced a variety of public relations materials including informational brochure, annual reports,
press announcements, and audio/visual presentation.

Client/Investor Relations
Extensive experience in maintaining various business contacts. Ranges from medical account collections and credit investigation to providing corporate
information to the investment community.

Professional *Teletek, Inc.*
Experience *Orion Broadcast Group, Inc.*
Director of Investor Relations
Promoted from administrative position to director of
investor relations program. Public relations with investment community, shareholder communication,
dissemination of financial information to various
parties. March 1981 to Present.

City Consumer Services, Inc.
Credit Investigator
Process applications for second mortgage lender.
Credit investigation, financial stability, loan closing.
July 1980 to March 1981.

Clinic Service Corporation
Account Representative
Collections, insurance processing for various med-
ical accounts.
June to August 1976/78; August to December 1979.

Education B.S.B.A.—*Finance*, University of Denver, 1980
University Scholar, Admissions Staff Assistant

RONALD
Address   **Phone**

Summary of Qualifications Extensive management experience with both government and private enterprise. Fifteen years experience in field of computer-assisted legal research. Broad experience in major areas of law with emphasis on contracts, both government and private. Broad general understanding of computers and their capabilities with emphasis on computer-assisted legal research systems.

Capabilities *General Management:* Planned, directed, and reviewed activities of three corporate departments; assisted in improvement and re-design of three major search and retrieval systems; established method for preparing legal materials for data entry; trained extensively, both employees and customers.

Contract Administration: Negotiated, drafted, and monitored contracts, including data conversion contract representing 1.2 million dollars. Negotiated and drafted license agreements with major publishers for exchange and use of computer-readable data.

Research: Performed legal research for thousands of employees throughout federal government on wide variety of legal issues using both traditional and computer-assisted research methods. Studied problem of using headnotes vis-a-vis full text and persuaded company to pursue full text.

Computers: Worked extensively with data processing personnel in design and operation of computer-assisted legal research systems.

Employment Supervisory Attorney-Advisor
Federal Legal Information Through Electronics (FLITE)
Denver, Colorado. 1974–1982

Science and Mathematics Teacher
Milwaukee Public Schools
Milwaukee, Wisconsin. 1973–1974

General Counsel, General Manager
Data Retrieval Corporation of America
Milwaukee, Wisconsin. 1966–1973

Bar Admission State of Wisconsin

Education J.D., 1968, Marquette University College of Law
B.A., 1965, Marquette University College of Liberal Arts
Major/Minor—Psychology/Philosophy

RICHARD

Address   **Phone**

Summary of   Project manager with extensive experience in
Qualifications energy resource industry, and special interest
                  in data management.

Capabilities   *Project Management:* Experienced in full range
                  of management functions including defining
                  program objectives, budgeting, supervision of
                  personnel, coordination of contractors, analyz-
                  ing data, evaluating results, and communicat-
                  ing recommendations. Experienced in coor-
                  dination with government regulatory agencies.
                  Fiscal Management: Includes budget develop-
                  ment, cost analysis, and budget administration.
                  Responsible for annual budgets exceeding one
                  million dollars.
                  Data Management: As exploration geologist,
                  was responsible for generating, organizing, and
                  evaluating large quantities of field data from
                  multiple sites.

Employment   Exploration Geologist—Uranium
                  Western Nuclear, Inc. (Subsidiary of Phelps
                  Dodge)
                  Lakewood, Colorado. 1969–1984
                  Exploration Geologist—Petroleum
                  Shell Oil Company
                  New Orleans, Louisiana. 1966–1969

Education   MS—Geology. 1966
                  University of Wyoming. Laramie, Wyoming
                  BS—Geology. 1963
                  Florida State University. Tallahassee, Florida

Personal   Married. Enjoy sailing, photography, outdoor
                  activities, antique clock collecting, and home
                  computing.

to sit loose to our expertise, venturing as novices beyond familiar competence.

My past two years' experience with computers has been a venture into the unknown. I am, as you sense, someone who enjoys words and ideas; I have few relationships with machines. Several years ago, I found myself reading the writings of Toffler, Naisbitt, and others who theorized on the new electronic information age; but I had not touched a computer and realized that I was hesitant to do so. Finally I managed to enroll in a couple of continuing-education, "Introduction to the Computer," courses. Had I been graded in the courses, I would have failed. But gradually I began applying a computer to my work. Here I could work and learn at my own pace. I asked my wife to read through manuals with me when I became impatient with the detail involved and got stuck. Today, I use a computer at work and another at home; I'm writing this text on a word processor. I still am not expert, but I do enjoy using the rudimentary skills I've gained as a novice.

It is in our interest, today, to nurture and honor ourselves as learners—whatever our level, whatever the skill. That way we can not only cope with social change, but grow with it as well. Others, such as our employers, also can benefit from our development; for organizations, just as individuals, may become bogged down in narrow competence.

Employing organizations, just as all other human enterprises, require and reward different sorts of competencies and behavioral styles. They invest in specialized skills. A construction-equipment rental company with which I have done consulting, for example, employs very few individuals in the analytical and influencing quadrants of Kolb's circle; most of the firm's activity is grounded in mechanical skill (understanding the equipment), and customer service (listening carefully to the needs of contractors so that they are provided with proper equipment, and dealing with their stress and anger when things go wrong). Sales is an activity that has received little emphasis, since this firm is one of very few regional sources for the equipment they rent. Analytical skills are concentrated in a few individuals such as the person who designed the company's computer system, and the credit manager who understands credit law and knows a good deal about the financial condition of major customers.

Organizations tend to perpetuate certain patterns of competence and style, both in their daily operations and as they hire new staff. Often there is a tendency to "clone the founders" of the organization and hire employees who will function comfortably with those already there. For example, if a company has had little involvement in sales, it is unlikely to employ many individuals who are accustomed to influencing others. Similarly, a firm founded by engineers will have a strong predisposition to employ other technical types.

But as an organization develops, management may decide that a fresh look at the competency styles of its employees is needed. It may be that the firm's business environment changes. For example, the appearance of new competitors may inspire increased interest in marketing and sales. Or it may be that key skills have become so concentrated in a few senior individuals that, even with compensatory insurance, the organization would be lost without them. (Ultimately, of course, every individual leaves every organization; the only variables are when the separation occurs, and how prepared everyone is for the occurrence.)

These are some good questions for an employer to share with his employees on a regular basis:

- What are two or three unique characteristics of your present responsibilities?
- What is your biggest problem on the job?
- What aspect of the job do you find most satisfying?
- In terms of training and/or additional support, what is the single most important thing you need?

Dialogue of this kind can help build a partnership for development.

In 1926 Alfred North Whitehead wrote, "The fixed person for the fixed duties, who in older societies was such a godsend, in the future will be a public danger" (Kolb, p. 183). So it is today

FIGURE 9

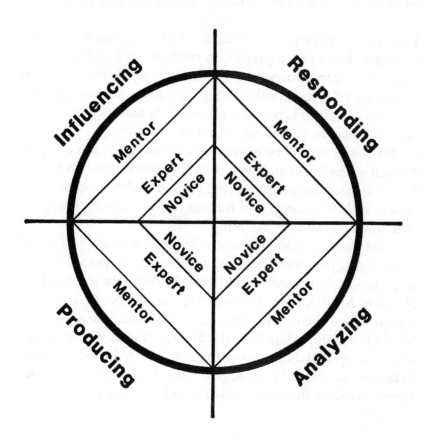

with many workers in specialized roles. As individuals, as organizations, and as a society, we no longer benefit from settling down in static skills. We need the ability to venture beyond the familiar. For, as Kenneth Boulding has observed, "When it comes to learning, nothing fails like success!"

In my efforts to help employees and employers prepare for changing job roles and competencies, I have integrated my career roles model with Kolb's Competency Circle. (*See Figure 9*.)

As you develop data on your own competencies and learning interests, it may be helpful to note them on this chart. Thinking of your whole range of life roles—worker, leisurite, volunteer—in which areas of competence do you function as novice, expert, mentor? Where are you growing? Where are you stale?

The value of this kind of reflection, as I've suggested, is to help us center down as we prepare to venture out into the marketplace. If we can understand the various facets of work investment—life role, career role, and competence—as they cohere in our lives at a given time, then we are likely to clarify factors that can be critical to purposeful direction.

So doing, we will be better able to concentrate our energies. For just as the laser can beam incredible power through sharply focusing the same quantity of light found in the florescent bulb, so it is with the energies of human beings. Concentrating our potentialities, we increase our power.

And there is another, more collective purpose to be served by clarifying personal direction. It is that the deeper we are able to understand ourselves as individuals, the more we may learn of others. Most people who work together can benefit from sharing questions such as those we have explored. The assessment format is less important than the process of discovering ways in which individual differences can contribute to building a team. In deeper, centered knowledge of ourselves, we may find new appreciation for the gifts of others, and new prospects for common growth.

CHAPTER 5

VENTURING OUT
Working in Response
to Need

*So it is too that in the eyes of the world it is dangerous
to venture. And why? Because one may lose. . . . And yet,
by not venturing, it is so dreadfully easy to lose that which
it would be difficult to lose in even the most venturesome
venture, and in any case never so easily, so completely as if
it were nothing . . . one's self.*

Søren Kierkegaard (Lowrie, tr., p. 52)

We have considered several approaches to clarifying the nature
and place of work in our lives. I have suggested that in seeking
a workplace, as in any other important venture, we ought to
begin by centering down and sorting out distinctive issues that
are vital to us as individuals. That way, we may not only concentrate our own energies, but also understand other individuals
at a deeper level as well.

But taking stock of ourselves is never more than the first step
in a process of productive growth. For whenever we venture to
make full use of our powers, ultimately we move beyond per-

sonal knowledge and intentions. As we grow in productivity, we pass into new realms of interaction where the substance and validity of whatever we initiate will require some response.

Every venture into the world of work entails an element of response. In his study of adult male development, *The Seasons of a Man's Life*, Daniel Levinson found that affirmation, by respected mentors in particular, was one of his subjects' most powerfully motivating work rewards. Meaningful work is reciprocal.

I have used the term "vocation" to describe deeply reciprocal work, wherein we are involved in the world on the basis of care. All of us, I believe, have the potential to discover a particular place where someone wants what we can do. Some may find that place outside paid employment. Many others will seek a new workplace where what they do for a living can correspond to what they live to do. Many of the methods and case examples of this chapter are intended to help support that kind of search.

But the discovery of vocation can't always be contrived. Sometimes it appears unexpected, almost independent of our intentions. Archie Hargraves, who became one of the great religious leaders of the 1960s civil-rights movement, describes an early experience when his career suddenly came alive as vocation:

> While I appreciated the intellectual framework provided by Christian faith, I did not make it a part of my gut and permit it to be incarnated through me, until an accident of grace occurred one day in East Harlem. I had been there three months desiring to minister, but people weren't having very much of my ministry. I had called on all the families in the block but hadn't reached first level as real friend.
>
> There was a sudden downpour of rain, and I ran to a stoop in front of one of the tenements to avoid getting wet. I heard a mighty roar and observed cascades of water rolling down the steps of the tenement and coming straight at me. Ignoring the peril to my health and safety, I jumped the waves and ran and flew up to the top floor, where it was raining as hard inside as outside. Sizing up the situation, I knocked on one of the tenement doors. A Mrs. Donohue opened the door of her

apartment. She had pots, pans, and pails all over the place in order to catch the water pouring from her ceiling.

I said, "Mrs. Donohue, isn't there something we can do?" She said, "What?" I said, "Let's get all the tenants together to stop this." Mrs. Donohue replied, "I'm Irish, I've lived here forty years. It's all the fault of those damn Italians who moved in about twenty years ago. I can't meet with such riffraff."

I went then to the next apartment and knocked. Mr. Moreno opened the door. Therein it was raining as hard inside as outside. A conversation similar to that which went on with Mrs. Donohue ensued. Mr. Moreno said in effect that he had lived in that building for twenty years, and the poor housing condition was the fault of "them niggers" who moved in about fifteen years ago. He would never sit down with "trash" with whom he had nothing in common.

Nothing to do but knock on the door of the third apartment. Mr. and Mrs. Wilkerson opened the door. The same condition obtained and virtually the same conversation ensued. They said in effect: We are West Indians. We have pride. But those southern Negroes don't. They are the cause of this mess. To meet with them would have no point and result in no solution.

Rebuffed at every turn, I went down the hall to the apartment of a southern Negro family, the Andersons. Their answer was in effect to blame the condition of a leaking, nay, a pouring roof, on the Puerto Ricans who had moved in three years before. They refused to meet with such "spic riffraff."

I then went to the apartment of a Puerto Rican family. Mrs. Rodriguez said: "We are from San Juan; the problem is with the rural people from Puerto Rico. And we don't mix with them."

To cut a long story short, I spent the next three months trying to get the families in this tenement together. I doubt that it was due to my persuasive ability but rather to annoyance at getting wet inside the house, that finally they got together in the apartment of Mrs. Donohue.

We recognized that we had a common problem, that we needed to lay out a common strategy, and to develop common action in which all would be involved in order to get a new roof.

Then somebody raised the question: "Reverend, we've

watched you. You got us together in spite of ourselves. We didn't want to. What is your racket? What are you trying to do with us? Do you want us to join that church with no members? We can't. We are everything. Roman Catholic! Jewish! Protestants of various hues and sortings! Some of us are even atheists!"

I didn't know how to answer at first. But I spoke of a need for people in the same space to overcome hostilities and work at common problem-solving. I then spoke of Ephesians which saw Christ as the breaker of the dividing wall. "We come," I said, "from many traditions. Why don't we work at recognizing our differences and our essential sameness, and select some tasks which need doing?"

The atheist said: "I never heard such nonsense. Show it to me in the Bible."

The roof got fixed the next week. But that tenement group continued to meet to study the Bible, assess and deal with problems, and grow deeper with each other. The group continued for three years, grew out toward the block, and finally into the neighborhood. My real discovery of faith came as it worked out in the context of a new covenant with that group.   (Charland, "Contracts," pp. 46–48)

Archie's experience illustrates the dimension of reciprocity in vocation. Whatever our life plans and private intentions, ultimately we find our way as we are met.

The incident also highlights another factor that is vital to meaningful employment: sensitivity to need. Archie grew in his workplace, which later became part of the renowned East Harlem Protestant Parish, as he learned to respond effectively to others' needs.

NEEDS ASSESSMENT

Most of us approach the labor market from the perspective of our own need—to find a job that pays well, to develop a secure career path, or perhaps (as in Archie's case) just to feel accepted as minister and friend. The agenda may vary, but our prime motive is the same. We want to meet our needs!

One instinctive response to this motive is to ask someone for a job. And, under conditions I'll discuss later, there is nothing wrong with doing that. There are, however, two serious disadvantages in beginning with this approach.

The first is that we are likely to be experienced as a burdensome dependent. Short of homicide and rape, probably no human act is as threatening as being asked for work. The individual whom we solicit obviously occupies a position of responsibility. Responsibility not only for himself but for others as well—current employees, children, ex-wives, and others. Much of this person's time and energies already are claimed by the manifold needs of these many others. When we approach someone so occupied as yet another prospective dependent—someone in need of work— we pour water on a drowning man. The response we elicit generally will be defensive withdrawal. Our would-be employer will pull in his horns, close up.

I have dramatized this process in career-development courses. At some unexpected point I ask for a moment of the students' time to share a personal concern. Much as I have enjoyed teaching at this school, I confide, I have just received notice that my position will end at the close of the current semester. I know that a number of the students are employed in positions of responsibility with local firms. Surely one of them will know of a possible job for me! "Joy, Bob, Ralph, will you see me after class, and let me know what's available?" . . . What follows is a good exercise in nonverbal communication. Joy and Bob are wide-eyed and pale. Ralph has sunk halfway beneath his desk. To describe these people as threatened is an understatement. To expect any of them to be able to offer help is a delusion. Much as they might genuinely wish me well and be willing to offer assistance, they cannot. For I have put them on the defensive, restricted their capacity to respond to me creatively, their ability to offer help.

Suppose, on the other hand, that I begin my job search from another side, and ask instead about what needs doing. Would you tell me something about your industry, Ralph? What are the principal challenges you face? Joy, could you share something about the company you work for? Where do you see them going in the next five years? Questions such as these enable others to help us. They open a process of investigation that can lead to a thorough assessment of industry and/or organization needs.

That brings us to the second disadvantage in beginning our approach to the labor market by asking for a job: the request is premature. Only after we have had an opportunity to understand the actual needs of prospective employers will we find ourselves in a position to know whether we can be of help to them. The process of seeking employment at a level of creativity and responsibility always begins with careful assessment of others' unmet needs.

Interviewing for information can help distinguish the felt needs of individuals and industries from our perception of their needs. That distinction—between perceived need and felt need—is basic to effective marketing of any kind, and never more critical than in marketing ourselves. Is there really an interest in what we have to offer? Often our very enthusiasm for an enterprise we value can blind us to the response of others. A small-business consultant I know finds this attitude among some of her clients who neglect to test their visions against reality, and thus often set themselves up for failure; she calls it "entrepreneurial euphoria."

Here is a set of questions I find helpful in this process of needs assessment:

Do I know what I want to do?
How well-informed is my judgment?
How deep is my commitment?
Am I in a position to make a free choice of my objective?
Or am I influenced primarily by the expectations of others, by economic exigencies, or by other extrinsic factors?

Am I equipped to accomplish my objective?
Professionally?
Personally?

If not, is it possible for me to acquire what is needed?

Is there a market for what I want to do?
Now?
In the near future?
If not, am I willing to:
Modify my objective?
Find another means to support it?

Finally, only as we spend time with persons in particular occupational groups will we discover whether we are likely to fit in there.

A few years ago I became a candidate for a new position as director of an educational association. I was interested in the association for a number of good reasons—in addition to needing the work! I'd had a long involvement in higher education and in the development of new programs involving innovative educational techniques. That was the purpose of the association as well. Furthermore, I was committed to remaining in Denver; the association was one of very few educational organizations based there. As I interviewed the association's board members individually, I also found that I liked them, and they seemed to respond well to me.

For a number of weeks I concentrated my job search on this organization. I visited the office, read reams of material, and prepared to meet with the entire board at their annual fall conference. Finally the time for the conference arrived, and I drove down to New Mexico to meet with the group. Only at that point, very gradually, did they and I become aware that I was not the person for the job.

Part of the problem had to do with their status as an organization. They had never employed a director. The organization was controlled by the board of directors and although, intellectually, they wanted to turn over much of their authority to someone else, they actually were not prepared to give up much control in order to do so. That was one source of unease. The other, which I could not understand until months later, was even more basic. This was an association of secondary-school teachers, and as a professional group they functioned quite differently from my colleagues in higher education. I still liked these people as individuals, but increasingly became aware that their rapid-fire style of creating new programs on the basis of very little reflection or research was foreign to the way I was accustomed to function. Their world of secondary-school teaching was, after all, dissimilar to teaching in a college. The common interests that had drawn us together were not as substantial as either party had assumed. And it had been necessary for us to spend considerable time together in order to discover that.

The aftermath of this episode is worth noting, in light of our earlier discussion of third-career mentoring. Finding themselves at an impasse, without an executive director, the board members dealt with the question of whether they really were ready to hire one. They contacted a long-time supporter of their association who recently had retired from a career in organization development. That man, in his sixties, spent the next year as a part-time, paid consultant to the association and helped the board carefully prepare for the eventual employment of a full-time, executive director. The needs of the association were met best by a good mentor.

For all these reasons, it is important to take our questions and intentions out into the marketplace. Only there can we come in sight of critical factors that will determine whether our objectives are viable.

There are some basic logistics that can support this process of needs assessment. The first is to be very clear and consistent with others as to whether we seek information and possible referral from them, or whether we seek paid employment with them. One of the worst counsels of some popular career-development literature is the suggestion that prospective employers should be approached through information interviewing. In addition to its fundamental dishonesty, such a strategy is impractical; one is apt to expose so much ignorance in the course of interviewing for information that it will be very difficult to appear expert later on. Conversely, a former employer or prospective employer who has some knowledge of our abilities and interests often is an excellent source of ideas about a workplace where we might fit better than in theirs.

One of Richard Germann's best suggestions is the use of a letter of approach to set the stage for a prospective interview (p. 84). Through such a letter, one can indicate the purpose of the interview (for information/referral and/or for employment), and share other important information such as how one received the person's name and a bit about one's own background. It's always best to arrange to call the individual and ask for an appointment of about a half hour at his office, rather than interview over the phone.

A résumé ought to be included with the letter only when one is seeking an interview for employment; résumés connote job search. In the case of information interviews, the résumé should be shared during the meeting and left behind for the person's files. It is important to prepare a brief, verbal description of one's background and interests—no longer than three or four minutes—and a set of questions based on previous research.

Whenever we learn of a promising place of employment through an information interview, it is appropriate to ask for referrals there. If the individual knows someone in a position of hiring authority, and feels some confidence in us, he will refer us to that person. It is courteous, then, to ask if we may use his name in the letter of approach and phone call for employment and/or further information that is to follow. It is important to seek interviews only with those who are in a position to offer good information (not just someone's uncle) and to whom, given our qualifications, we can pose no threat. A referral to someone in personnel is tantamount to an expression of no confidence or, at any rate, caution. Personnel officers are buffers and channels between managers who hire and job applicants. While there is nothing lost by adding our résumé to the multitude in their files, it is far more effective to persist in seeking avenues to someone who actually can make an employment decision.

Following an interview of any kind, we should send a note

of appreciation with a review of what we learned about possible directions and the courses of action we intend to follow. If there is a feeling of good rapport, we ought to keep in touch with the individual from time to time—not only in the context of our own ambitions, but also offering something in return, such as sending an interesting article one comes across in a journal. Effective information interviewing is not only a method of needs assessment, but also a way of building relationships within the vital networks of professional life.

NETWORKING

Several years ago a Harvard sociologist, Mark Granovetter, surveyed a group of individuals who had assumed new professional and technical positions. Granovetter was interested in how the jobs had been acquired. He found that only 10 percent or so had been publicized in classified advertisements, and that only another 10 percent had come from recruiters and other agencies. No less than 75 percent of the new jobs resulted from face-to-face contacts within professional networks. I see the same pattern every week. The majority of people who find new and interesting work opportunities in fields about which they care turn them up through direct encounter with individuals who already are at work there.

"Networks" take many forms in our society. Some have developed from high technology. Modems linking computers have made it possible for many individuals, each with a small and specialized pool of data, to share information via their individual terminals, rather than rely on a single central repository. Data sharers are an important, new kind of network (Cornish, p. 24).

But networks of other kinds are not new. They have always been a part of our lives. Some are quite specialized, such as the large group of ruddy-cheeked people I ran into the other night at our Friends Meeting House. It turned out that they were the Colorado Cavers, an organization of spelunkers who get together one night each month to exchange whatever it is that cavers share. Alvin Toffler and others have noted the dramatic increase in special-interest networks of this kind. They represent a strong, pervasive trend toward diversification in our society.

Professional networks function just as the other groups we've noted, but less visibly. Persons involved in a common profession often meet and talk, for a variety of reasons. For one thing, as illustrated in my experience with the secondary-school teachers, occupational groups are essentially social groups. Chiropractors, to cite another example, are a decidedly homogeneous group. Some research based on the Strong-Campbell Interest Inventory has suggested that, compared to physicians, individuals who have worked steadily and successfully as chiropractors are very entrepreneurial. And the most reliable indication of whether you or I might fit well in the chiropractic field is not a measurement of our abilities (such as a gift for tugging necks or kneading backs), but of our general, human interests—how similar they are to the interests of chiropractors. On the basis of common characteristics such as these, people in the same occupational group—even competitors—generally form a network.

Sometimes an occupational network will become quite visible in the form of a professional association. Meetings will be scheduled every month or so, officers elected, etc. Occasionally, a professional association will grow into a large, well-staffed and funded organization that actively seeks new members. But more often the association will choose to remain small and informal. Many are so exclusive as to be secretive. The founders of one association, in the field of industrial training, were remarkably successful in recruiting new members. It wasn't long before their monthly meetings were filled to overflowing. Then they began to realize that the majority of those who attended were there simply to buttonhole others for jobs. The meetings became little more than flesh markets. Finally the founders withdrew from their own organization and developed a new, informal association in which they once again could share professional concerns and give attention to their own growth.

These observations suggest the close relationship of professional networks to the processes of employment. Granovetter's study simply confirmed what others have estimated many times:

the great majority of professional and technical positions are filled through personal contacts. These contacts are developed through informal, professional networks.

Indeed, if we look beyond employment to consider other forms of social intercourse, we find the same dynamic operative. Most of us in our social lives meet the people we date and/or marry through informal contacts—friends of friends, fellow students, members of our religious group and the like. Occasionally we notice advertisements for agencies that offer to facilitate the process of introduction—videotape-dating bureaus, for instance. But most of us never call them; we meet new friends through networks of others we already know.

Employment in the professions functions the same way. Most organizations that find a need for personnel look for new people within the networks of those they know—or of those who are known by their acquaintances. Only as a last resort do they move beyond their informal professional networks to formal channels of introduction such as classified ads and recruiting firms.

Ads and recruiters are the employers' counterpart to the videotape-dating bureau. There is, of course, nothing wrong with responding to them effectively. Sometimes excellent jobs are found through the want ads. And executive search firms can be a good source of positions similar to those which one already has held. (See Appendix.) But in practice the most effective methods to find a workplace—paid, or volunteer—are based on our distinctiveness as individuals who have unique gifts to share. They are based on self-marketing through needs assessment.

o Maria graduated from college five years ago with a major in marketing. Her first job was in retail sales management for a large department store in Tucson. She left it to return to Denver, and then worked for a small home-furnishings store downtown. When the economy turned bad, Maria's job ended and she took the opportunity of unemployment to determine what it was she really wanted to do.

It was evident, as we worked together in assessment, that Maria had enjoyed using her training in marketing. And it was clear that she had tired of retail sales. In addition to its long hours and low pay, she found the work meaningless. We reviewed test results and values-clarification exercises, and talked at length about her background in western Colorado, growing up in a Greek-speaking community on a sheep ranch. Maria came alive when she described her childhood in that community. Her dark eyes glowed. Clearly she had no desire to spend the rest of her life on a ranch. But she still held part ownership in the family ranch and enjoyed going back at busy seasons to help out. There was something about her ranching background and her upbringing in that group of Greek sheep ranchers that continued to hold meaning for her.

As we talked, she thought of a national wool-growers' association in Denver that recently had changed leadership. She didn't know the new director, but had acquaintances who did. She did know that conditions for the ranchers were not getting easier and sensed they could benefit from more sophisticated marketing strategies. Maria wondered if there might be opportunities to work there.

She first did some investigation of the association and its recent history. Maria learned why the previous director had left and more about the new one. She did some library research on marketing in other food industries, and reviewed a recent advertising campaign sponsored by the association. Maria then called up the association director and asked for an appointment to discuss marketing needs in the sheep industry. Perhaps there were opportunities for her to serve the industry through the association, utilizing her background in marketing, sheep ranching, and retail sales of textiles. If not, perhaps the director could put her in touch with others who would know of openings elsewhere. They did meet and, not to my surprise, the director began thinking of ways to find a place for Maria, her abilities and background in marketing, and her genuine interest in their industry. She is working there today.

Maria's approach to seeking employment through needs assessment introduces broader dimensions of self-marketing.

SELF-MARKETING

Marketplaces are found in all societies large enough to have specialized work roles. These societies must provide in some way for the exchange of goods and services; traditionally, this was done face to face. In the industrial era of our recent past, as Alvin Toffler notes, the scale and scope of economic activity grew enormously, with the result that producers and consumers of goods and services were separated.

It was in this era, during the last three centuries, that the market took on a life of its own. Producers and consumers who could not trade in person now were able to communicate through market media such as merchandise marts, advertising, and stock exchanges. The process of economic transaction became much more complex and sophisticated. "Marketing" is the modern art of facilitating that process.

Whenever any of us addresses the market seeking a workplace of any kind, we can benefit by paying attention to the "market value" of what we are prepared to offer. For that is the way needs and the means of satisfying them are communicated in a large, complex society such as ours. We begin by focusing on what we can supply. Some of the questions that can assist us in this process are similar to those we would ask of any other product, any other outcome of someone's productive capacity.

- Where is there a demand ("market") for what we have to offer? What are the needs of that market segment where the product is, or might be, in demand?
- How does the product appear in the marketplace? Is it "packaged" in an appropriate, attractive form?
- How much does the product cost? Does the proposed

price communicate the potential benefits it offers?

- How does the product compare to others in the marketplace? Are there many similar products to be found? Is the product so novel that no one is likely to understand or appreciate what it offers?

- Has the product outlived its "product life?" That is, if it once held value in the marketplace, have circumstances changed to the degree that the product has lost its appeal? Could the product be modified in some way so as to increase interest in it?

- What factors can be expected to influence demand for the product? How stable has demand been in the past? What are some of the most important characteristics (such as geography, demography, income) of sectors in the marketplace where the product appears to be in demand?

Marketing, as the process through which questions such as these are resolved, comprises two principal activities: *product development* and *promotion*. Some economic enterprises emphasize the former and others the latter. A company that has introduced a revolutionary, "super computer" has employed two-thirds of its two-hundred employees in research and development, refining the new product; its top officials have been responsible primarily for raising capital to support product development. Very few computers have been manufactured, and none as yet have been sold. The prime focus of this organization is product development.

Another company I know manufactures and distributes tape-recorded books and magazine articles. Here, product development receives much less emphasis than promotion. There is some attention given to selecting what materials to record, and careful management of the process of production. But the primary concern of this organization is finding new markets for the materials. For example, they are about to open a distributorship in Europe.

Here again it can be helpful to apply fundamental principles of marketing to ourselves. For some of us, at certain periods in life, it may be best to concentrate on the quality of our resources. In other times and circumstances, we will need to emphasize promotion, getting people involved in what we have to offer. As individuals, just as with organizations, effective marketing requires not only that we give attention to both product development and promotion, but that we appreciate which one deserves emphasis at a given time.

The ability to relate needs and interests on the one hand to goods and services available on the other helps societies function productively. One need only observe the operations of many centrally planned economies to understand why countries such as The Peoples Republic of China and Tanzania are attempting to re-establish free market systems of exchange.

There are sectors of our own society where we need better channels of market information. Our American economy is increasingly segmented into regional markets with some growing rapidly and others just as rapidly in decline. Yet we have had no systematic method of communicating information about job opportunities in Houston to the unemployed people of Youngstown, Ohio.

The efficient communication of supply/demand information is critically important to many professions caught up in change. It is one facet of a larger, challenging task of remarketing skills in midstream. Today, the transformation of a single occupational role within an individual lifetime is a widespread phenomenon. One can think of many examples of persons whose job titles have remained constant but whose duties have changed drastically. There is the chief of police in an energy boom town. Ten years ago he knew all of his constituents personally. Today he copes with a rapidly rising crime rate and a ritualized, impersonal professional role. Or the college dean who once simply assisted students and faculty as he administered a rather static set of programs. Now, in a time of eroding enrollment, the same person, with the same title, is likely to find much of his time spent marketing and managing a kaleidoscope of new programs. Many bank executives entered that field to work with numbers and people in a subdued and stable environment. Under deregulation they are required to make cold calls and sales. Hospital administrators find themselves engaged in advertising campaigns. The list could go on.

Nowhere in my experience is this process of role transformation as pronounced as in the profession of librarian. Until recently, librarians performed a rather stolid function as custodians for repositories of data. One went to see the librarian for assistance in locating a certain increment of information; the librarian pointed to a shelf. One encountered the librarian also if the material borrowed from the repository came overdue; librarians collected book fines. Or, if one became too exuberant in the presence of the collected data, librarians said "Sh!"

Today, under the impact of an explosion in information technology, the role of librarian has undergone cataclysmic change. With the present rapid development of electronic data processing and the impending application of communication technology to information transfer, an entire new profession is emerging: information management. Organizations of all kinds are caught up in the convergence of telecommunications and computer technology. No longer dependent on the static collections of traditional libraries, they now want access to many sources of information all over the world. And the help they need can't be found in the traditional librarian, but only in a new kind of information professional—one who is prepared to serve as facilitator and mediator with a whole range and complex of dynamic information systems.

Can those who have served as librarians now become the information managers that the modern age requires? That is a question many administrators of library science schools are asking.* On the one hand, they note, the intellectual challenge in adapting to the new role is not great. Traditional, professional education in library science is an excellent foundation for information management. One can update skills with a few computer

---

*Ben Franckowiak, former Dean of the Graduate School of Librarianship and Information Management at the University of Denver, is a leader in this group and the source of much of my knowledge about the changing role of librarians.

science courses and become qualified to function as an information manager.

At a personal level, the change may be much more difficult. Librarians have been nurtured in a heretofore stable, closed environment. The world of information managers, especially in industry, is more innovative and fluid. As automation and cutbacks in federal funds have curtailed employment in traditional, public-sector library jobs, one might expect to see librarians flocking to enter the new information roles. But many who sense the difference in environment and are disturbed by it shrink from the change. Recently one urban library was forced to eliminate fifty professional librarian positions. The word went out to employees six months in advance of the date for termination. During those six months, only two of the librarians left their jobs for new positions. The others simply waited to be let go. A number of them continue to work for the library in clerical positions, having traded tremendous losses in salary and status for the comfort of a familiar working environment.

Self-marketing skills can help individuals live more productively in the midst of circumstances such as these—not merely undergoing change, but growing through it as well. There are, however, several important features of marketing that should be considered in applying the process to ourselves.

The first is that marketing is not the same activity as selling. Many career guidance, self-help books teach methods of promoting oneself through techniques of hard sell, as in powerful clothes. (One of my colleagues recently commented on our students' style of dress for employment interviews: "Are those guys all wearing the same suit?") Selling, the process of persuading a customer to follow a preselected course of action—to buy from us—clearly has its place in the world. Selling generates economic activity, and can be a valuable endeavor. Some people find that their métier.

Selling *oneself*, however, almost always diminishes us as persons. It may lead to a chameleonlike character orientation: "I am as you desire me!" (Fromm, p. 75ff.) This mode of addressing the marketplace does nothing for personal character, and it also is ineffective. Bent on appearing pleasing to a wide variety of prospective employers, we are unable to communicate our distinctive personal qualities and professional skills to any of them.

Trying to sell ourselves may spawn other forced and false behaviors—especially if self-promotion doesn't come easy. A young man who has read a number of career-development books described a job interview he had just completed. Ned is a rather shy, retiring accountant. Trying to prepare himself for the frightening prospect of employment interviews, he had studied a book that advocates aggressive, if not manipulative, interviewing tactics. The result was bizarre. "And so, to clinch the deal," he recalled, "I leaned across his desk and said, 'So you agree that I am the ideal candidate for this job?'" I can't remember how he described the interviewer's response, but it wasn't positive! Clearly, the person had felt manipulated and confused by this kind of action from an otherwise diffident accountant. The hard-sell can diminish both our personal being and our market value.

Marketing, on the other hand, begins from our own distinctiveness—what it is that we have and want to offer—and proceeds to identify as clearly as possible the roles and organizations through which we might function. Marketing is a way of matching carefully what we can supply with those places where what we have to offer is likely to be in demand. Marketing is a way of helping us find our way to a place we are needed.

Second, we should consider the relationship of market demand to value. The market, as I have suggested, provides a good medium for correlating the supply of existing goods and services with current levels of interest and demand. The language of that process is price. People will pay for what they need and/or find of interest.

As the lingua franca of a complex economy where most of us cannot deal firsthand in goods and services we understand, price serves a useful purpose. We can communicate through the language of price. But price does not constitute value. All kinds of goods and services may have worth which the market cannot measure.

o I remember a high-school friend, a rather nondescript fellow when I first knew him in grade school, who became an accomplished saxophone player. The sax was very big in those days, and Dan was much in demand by dance bands. He signed my yearbook, I recall, with a characteristic musical notation; Dan's young-adult identity was bound up with his saxophone. Another contemporary was my guitar teacher, Rolly. When I first knew Rolly, he was one of a very few professional guitarists in Minneapolis, and barely afloat financially. He loved his instrument, however, as Dan did his, and was thoroughly invested in his teaching and playing. Within a period of about two years, largely due to the influence of Elvis Presley, popular music tastes were transformed. Gone was the saxophone, along with romantic ballads. The guitar became America's favorite instrument. Rolly bought a store to sell guitars, hired his former students to give lessons, and became a wealthy man. I don't know what happened to Dan. But I hope he still is playing the saxophone somewhere, for he was very good, and the instrument was an important part of his life. And I know for certain that the real value of Rolly and Dan as creative individuals who enjoyed entertaining others through their music is constant, independent of the relative popularity of saxophone or guitar.

One of the worst consequences of confusing market worth and value is measuring oneself by salary. A year ago, I worked with a man who made $45,000 in his last job. When the job was eliminated, he set out to find another that would pay him the same wage. Type of work or field of endeavor meant little, compared to salary. He was a $45,000-a-year man! After nine months of unemployment, his job search was successful, and now once again he is at one with his history; his new job pays $45,000 a year.

Compensation, in fact, can take many forms, and the criteria for success can't always be equated with salary. Bernie Brillstein, John Belushi's manager, suggested that the late comedian's final self-destructive drug binge may have been set off by the rejection of a screenplay he had coauthored. The rejection was accompanied by an offer from the same studio of $10–12-million dollars for performing four additional comic movie roles during the next two years. Clearly, money carries very different meaning for different individuals.

John Kenneth Galbraith, fifteen years ago, wrote with great insight about money and motivation in *The New Industrial State*. The importance of money declines, he said, as opportunities increase to identify with the aims of an organization and/or to influence it. Paradoxically, those who enjoy that kind of identification and influence also generally are best paid!

But not always. Many of the world's most influential work roles—such as teacher—are underpriced, partly perhaps because of their intrinsic rewards. And those who find their vocation in helping others grow, in creating new art forms, in working for social justice, or in many other endeavors that may not pay well, ought never to measure themselves by their paychecks.

Neither should those who could benefit from "lateral growth." People often are disinclined to move to another position at the same level as the one they have held. They like to move up instead. But a lateral move, or even down a notch, sometimes can provide the time and space one needs to cultivate a craft. The automatic rejection of lateral moves has traditionally been a male problem—a product of sex-role conditioning. Like nicotine addiction, it is a problem shared increasingly by our sisters.

One of the most helpful contributions of feminist psychology (e.g., Carol Gilligan, *In a Different Voice*) to a new understanding of work is the suggestion that our traditional, male "ladder of success" ought to be replaced by a matrix something like a web. (*See Figure 10.*) Organizations as well as individuals could benefit by encouraging career moves in all directions, on the basis of interdependent interest and intrinsic need, and not just criteria of market demand such as salary.

Doris Drury, a noted economist, summarized the discussion best in terms of her own profession during a 1985 conference:

FIGURE 10

Not 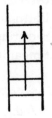   but

"An economist can tell us the price of everything, and the value of nothing!"

Finally, the marketplace may not tell us what we ought to know about needs of the future. History abounds with instances of opportunities lost for lack of foresight: the agricultural Indians, for example, who found horses that had escaped from the Spaniards, and ate them! By contrast, an indigent group living on roots and berries had the good sense to capture, tame, and ride the horse. That tribe developed a flourishing Plains culture (Farb, p. 29).

Today, under conditions of exponential change, most of us are hard-pressed to see some of the most critical, formative, trends of the future. One of my students in a seminar on career futures shook his head when he recalled having sold the only Moped dealership in our part of the country three weeks before the 1973 Arab oil embargo!

The process and pace of social change by which industries emerge and die, and the difficulty of determining their direction, have sparked a whole "new" industry today—the business of prognostication.

It is interesting to view the futures industry in historical perspective, for futurists certainly have been busy before. Biblical prophets always faced the problem of identification with "false prophets" of one sort or another. Jesus was surrounded by individuals who looked for signs portending change. His admonition that none would be given other than the sign of Jonah (who was himself a sign) suggests that human beings themselves are the principal determiners of future events (Luke 11).

Inappropriate reliance on authority, based on our human proclivity for finding someone else to provide direction, is a constant hazard in times of great change. Some people seek signs of change in Biblical prophecy misconstrued as prediction. That desire prompted the apocalyptic writings of New Testament times and a plethora of doomsday-oriented religious groups in eighteenth-century America, as well as during other periods of transition.

The same dependence may account in part for the popularity of secular futurists. Books that purport to identify future trends enjoy unprecedented sales. John Naisbitt notes that "Membership in the World Future Society grew from 200 in 1967 to well over 49,000 in 1979, and the number of popular and professional periodicals devoted to understanding or studying the future has dramatically increased from 12 in 1965 to over 122 in 1978" (p. 18). His own book, *Megatrends*, became the number one nonfiction best seller in the nation.

This development is constructive insofar as it prepares more of us to function more effectively as prophets—discerning the issues of greatest importance to us and taking action on the basis of our vision. But it is debilitating to the degree it encourages reliance on the prescience of others. For broad analysis of societal trends doesn't do justice to our unique needs and gifts as individuals. Furthermore, under conditions of exponential change, future-forecasting is something less than an exact science. There is no infallible source of information on that which has not transpired. Alvin Toffler's *Future Shock* preceded *The Third Wave* by only a dozen years. Yet, *Future Shock* makes no mention of the microprocessor—the linchpin of the postindustrial era which is the principal subject of *The Third Wave* (Evans, p. 110). Similarly, neither Toffler nor any other futurist predicted the massive entry of women into the American paid labor force during the 1970s: perhaps the most significant development of that decade. Futurists are fallible. In the last analysis, we can expect no better indicator of the future than the sign of Jonah. Only as our own best visions of the future are embodied in action can the tasks that will form the future actually get done. Exercise 3, based on the futures invention work of Warren Ziegler (see Appendix) will help us do that. It is the first of several instruments to help us "think upstream" for ourselves.

There are several other resources for envisioning future developments that are available to any of us. One of the most reliable is demographic data. A great deal can be surmised about the future simply on the basis of how many people were born when, and where. For example, as we have noted, our society contains an immense population bulge comprised of those who were born in a twenty-year period of economic growth following World War II. The progress of this "baby-boom" cohort continues to have great impact on all our social institutions—something like a pig in a python! Interestingly, a corresponding bulge in the population of Mexico follows immediately after ours, suggesting increased interaction between our labor forces during the last years of this century.

This observation about US–Mexican population patterns can illustrate a useful way to envision future trends. If we write down a single phenomenon about which we feel some certainty (and demographic information is among the most reliable), we can extrapolate from that single development others that are likely to follow. (*See Figure 11.*) For example, (1) the population increase among working-age Mexicans at a time when the number of US workers will wane portends several related developments: (2) additional immigration, sanctioned and welcomed by the US, of Mexican workers; (3) possible reliance of US industry on unskilled labor, available in large supply, as an alternative to further mechanization; (4) possible attempts to finance a troubled US Social Security System through tax payments by Mexican workers in this country; (5) increased bilingual education on both sides of the border, etc. The developments might be diagrammed through this design, which can be used for a quick scan of any number of issues.

Another useful way to envision future developments is to think about forces counter to prevailing trends. Growth occurs

ENVISIONING THE FUTURE

Consider the year 2000—that benchmark for the new age of Buck Rogers. Close your eyes for a few minutes, and imagine the year 2000 the way you used to envision it as a child. Fantastic images fill the Saturday matinee screen in your mind. What do you see?

When you have opened your eyes, consider this. The year 2000 is only x years away! To put that fact in perspective, think back the same number of years and jot down a few notes on your life then. Where were you working, or in school? What was your community like? Your home and family?

Close your eyes once more, and envision life in the year 2000. What would you like to see—in your life, work, community, family? Give yourself some quiet space and time to call up some clear images of your hopes for yourself and others in the year 2000. When you've finished, make some notes on what you saw in that scenario.

Goals

In the space below, please write down some of your thoughts concerning personal and professional goals, both long and short range, which could help bring your vision for the year 2000 into being.

	Personal	*Professional*
10 years		
5 years		
6 months		

FIGURE 11

RAMIFICATIONS CHART

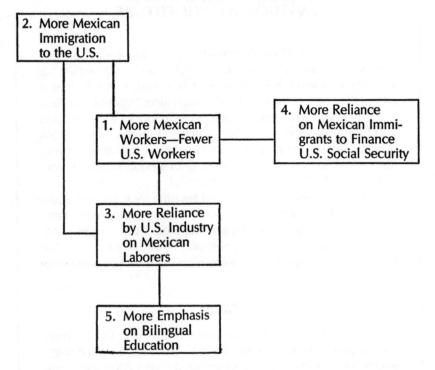

most often in the form of a recumbent S. For a time, the growth is all in one direction; then a countervailing force impedes it, until the process of growth resumes, but at a lower level. The typical process looks like Figure 12. For example, in looking at population growth in Colorado, with a concomitant expectation that its interstate highway along the Front Range will be fourteen lanes wide by the end of the century, one can anticipate some other factors such as effective protests by environmental groups and/or the development of a light-rail public transportation system that will impede the trend. This is an interesting way to consider a variety of other issues, such as the proliferation of nuclear weapons, or the growth of Mexico City to a projected population of 36 million by the end of the century. What factors are likely to intervene?

FIGURE 12

Figure 13 is a chart that depicts employment trends. Clearly, information-based jobs lead all the rest. But what about counter-vailing factors such as information overload? Will we, one day, have our fill of sophisticated data-processing technology and long for something like the soil?

Yet another way to organize our ideas about developments in the future is through a system of concentric circles that I call the P Complex. Begin by writing down all of the possible developments you can envision in a particular field. Think of this as the list of the *possible*. Include everything that comes to mind, no matter how far-fetched it may seem. Then, separately, write down those items from the first list that seem *plausible*. From this second list, note the items that appear *probable*. Finally, in another separate list, identify all the items that seem *preferable*. The lists should represent a configuration like that shown in Figure 14.

It may be interesting, for example, to reflect upon how our society will cope with the aging of our baby-boom cohort. We know that their sheer numbers already are a source of strain. One of my thirty-five-year-old clients shook his head and reflected on the competition he experienced in trying to find a job. "All my life, I've been in crowds," he lamented. "Double shifts in grade school, triple shifts in high school, trying to buy a house, get a job—always in the presence of all these other people. Sometimes it seems there are just too many of us!"

We already have considered the impact of this group on pension systems. An additional, complicating factor has to do with changes in lifestyle. Between 1960 and 1980, the number of "single households" in the United States increased 66 percent. Where will all the aged, single people live? Will they return to

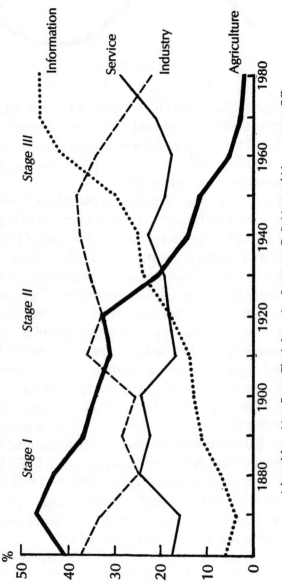

FIGURE 13

FOUR SECTOR AGGREGATION OF THE
U.S. WORK FORCE BY PERCENT 1860–1980
(Using median estimates of information workers)

Information

Service

Industry

Agriculture

Stage I   Stage II   Stage III

%
50
40
30
20
10
0

1880   1900   1920   1940   1960   1980

Adapted from Marc Porat, The Information Economy: Definition and Measurement, Office
of Telecommunications Special Publication 77 12(1), May 1977

FIGURE 14

THE P COMPLEX

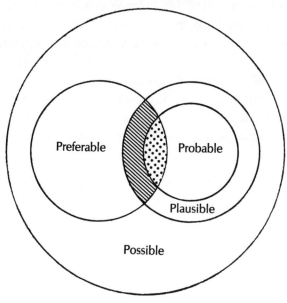

the homes now being designed and marketed for "mingles"—large master bedrooms and separate baths for unaffiliated, young adults who live together out of economic necessity? That is one possibility for the largest sphere.

Another, which I've yet to see anyone really develop, came to me last year when my alma mater died. Yankton College was but one of hundreds of small private colleges scattered throughout the countryside of America. Now that the baby-boom cohort has passed young adulthood, a number of these schools will not survive as institutions for the young. Not even the baby boomlet—children of the massive cohort, sometimes designated the "yuppy puppies"—can save them. But what about converting some of the dormitories to residential facilities for senior citizens, and remarketing the colleges as multigeneration learning communities? That could be an economically efficient, life-enriching solution to two troubling social needs.

Social inventions are born, as Naisbitt's research has confirmed, at the grassroots level. They are likely to develop among those who care about problems that conventional wisdom can't resolve, and who also are able to think about the problems in new ways. But Naisbitt's image of "windows of opportunity" into the future is overstated. New directions first appear as faint glimmerings, something on the scale of cracks in the siding. Those that truly open new ways are proven only as individuals act on their dreams. And ventures of that kind require a perspective that not only views market conditions realistically but also leaves room for inventive vision and personal concern.

* * *

FINDING EMPLOYMENT: TWO EXAMPLES

How are professional positions filled? It is probably more accurate to ask how they are formed since, as we have seen, most meaningful workplaces are co-created.

Employment decisions are made on the basis of three criteria: competence, commitment, and compatibility. Does the prospective employee have most of the skills required? How much does the person seem to care about what we do? And, can we get along?

Employment interviewing essentially is a process of resolving these questions. We might think of the factors in the relation shown in Figure 15. If exceptional qualities of competence, commitment, or compatibility appear, allowances are made for deficiencies in other spheres. Both parties to the process will have legitimate concerns, and it is important to take time to work them through. That's why most professional positions are filled only after long dialogue in a series of interviews.

> o Mike's experience includes most of the factors that characteristically manifest themselves as an individual sets out in search of a workplace.
>
> Mike is a former journalist whose early career was transient. He rose in his profession through jobs in a number of cities, finally becoming managing editor of a major daily newspaper. Mike married soon after, and he and Sue decided to settle in their city where she could build her interior design business as Mike continued his career in journalism.
>
> When I met Mike, he had resigned from the paper. Long hours and constant pressure finally had got to him. He was tired of getting up at 4:30 A.M. and getting home, on a good day, at 6:00 P.M. in the evening; it was time for a change.
>
> Mike knew that he wanted to remain in the field of communications, and was aware of some important issues he wanted to address. Most large organizations in his community seemed unsophisticated when it came to the news media.

FIGURE 15

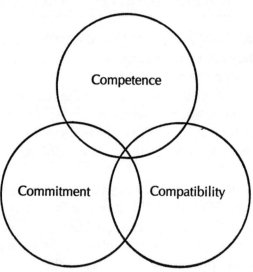

They failed to take advantage of opportunities for local coverage of their activities; and, when something went wrong in their lives, often they found themselves victimized by sensationalists in the press. Mike wanted to introduce a new level of public relations in his community, where it seemed to lag far behind the professional quality found in other cities where he had worked. But he wasn't at all sure that he wanted to run a one-man consulting firm. He needed to find an employer.

He began talking with colleagues and friends in the field, not to ask them for employment but to compare notes on the needs he perceived and to ask for suggestions as to where he might develop a place from which to address them. One of his contacts was the manager of marketing for a firm that had sought some public relations services from a well-known local advertising agency. The agency, it turned out, had little use for public-relations professionals, based on its experience with local firms; but, his contact commented, this was one of several requests received recently for public-relations services. They were beginning to consider whether, in fact, they ought to establish a public-relations division of their own— if they could do so without damaging their professional identity and reputation.

Mike received a referral to one of the partners in the ad agency, and sent him a letter in which he described his background in communications and the kind of service he hoped to develop. He indicated who had referred him to the agency and said that he would call in a few days to ask for an appointment to discuss a possible interest in his ideas.

There followed a series of several meetings, first with the partner to whom he had been referred, then with both partners, and finally with the entire professional staff of the agency. Part of the first meeting included a candid discussion of local public-relations activities; the ad agency held a negative view of the field and Mike found it helpful to describe in some detail how public-relations professionals in other cities functioned. At the end of the meeting, he received an invitation to another the following week, and an assignment. The ad agency had received a request from one of its clients, a child-care organization, to develop a media-relations contingency plan for possible emergencies such as an outbreak of illness in the facility, or the kidnapping of a child.

Mike prepared a plan, based partly on conversations with his sister who is an experienced school administrator. In addition, he put together an outline of key issues for consideration and steps to be followed should the agency wish to proceed further with the process of establishing a public-relations division.

At the end of the second meeting, Mike still had no offer of employment, but he was given a contractual consulting assignment with one of the agency's accounts. A subsequent meeting was planned, but not scheduled, as the firm was preoccupied with an impending move to new offices. They asked Mike for professional references and indicated they would contact them before getting together again.

Mike began work on his consulting assignment and he

also applied for another position—as manager of the new local office of a large public-relations firm based in another city. He was flattered to find himself one of two final candidates for this position from a pool of six hundred respondents to a classified ad. The process of interviewing for this position was much more formal than the first and included the administration of psychological tests and a consultation with an industrial psychologist.

The next two weeks were rough. Mike heard nothing from either prospective employer. He sent a friendly letter to each, summarizing the basis of his interest in each position and indicating the contributions he believed he could make, and he called each employer once during the second week to ask how the process was proceeding. In addition, he talked further with some of his friends in the field. In those conversations, he learned two items of great interest. The first firm had not yet contacted any of his references. And the second, it developed, was involved in negotiations to acquire a local public-relations agency—a possibility that had not been shared with him. A staff member of that agency was reported to be the other candidate to head their office; since this person already had working relationships with the local clients, he appeared to have a strong inside track for the job.

Mike resisted the inclination to make more calls, and invested his energies in talking with other friends and colleagues about his career interests and the local market. He also worked on his consulting projects and tried to spend time in activities unrelated to work. Finally, the first firm called. The reasons for their delay, the partner indicated, were not only the move but also an insidious, nagging reservation about Mike. Much as they liked him, and good as his references had turned out to be, they were bothered by the fact that Mike never had served on the staff of an established public-relations firm. Did he, in fact, have the knowledge necessary to establish the kind of operation that could enhance their firm?

Mike was tempted to defend himself on the spot; after

all, he had managed a newspaper with a staff of two hundred (eight times the size of this agency's staff), and had dealt with major firms as an editor. But he decided simply to acknowledge their concern, and asked to address it at a meeting they now scheduled.

How could he respond to their concern about his qualifications? He had no better references than the people they already had consulted. He decided that he would take to the next meeting a copy of the job description from his second prospective employer, the established, out-of-state, public-relations firm. The ad agency knew that he was a final candidate for that position. Now, he would review the qualifications the other firm saw as important—represented in the job description—and candidly assess with them how his skills matched up.

As it developed, that tactic was unneeded. The "night before the wedding" anxiety of the partners dissipated; what seemed to matter was that they had been able to communicate candidly with Mike; that helped them to confirm their comfort with him as a colleague. During the course of a two-hour meeting with the partners, other members of the staff interrupted repeatedly as they brought in additional consulting projects they wanted Mike to review. At lunch, Mike was invited to join the firm.

Finding meaningful employment usually is an exercise in needs assessment, addressing places and problems where we wish to be involved. The process requires that we look long and clear within ourselves, and also at the landscape of life around us. Ultimately it calls us out into the marketplace of others' concerns, testing our "working hypotheses" against the needs they feel. At every stage, it is an enterprise that summons all the patience, caring, and courage which every venture in faith requires.

V. S. Naipaul in *A Bend in the River* describes the task of seeking work through the eyes of a young Indian. Having grown up on the east coast of Africa and emigrated to England, the young man finds that he doesn't fit established British institutions. His university placement office with its standard schedule of job interviews delivered to applicants in official envelopes is not the resource he needs.

> It wasn't easy after I left the university. I still had to get a job, and the only thing I knew now was what I didn't want to do. I didn't want to exchange one prison for another. People like me have to make their own jobs. It isn't something that's going to come to you in a brown envelope. The job is there, waiting. But it doesn't exist for you or anyone else until you discover it, and you discover it because it's for you and you alone.

How is meaningful employment found? Sometimes it finds us, through a visceral response to need.

Another of my clients discovered a deep sense of vocation outside his career in technical sales, in an arresting experience as a volunteer:

> o I became aware of CONTACT: Lifeline of Denver while looking through the front of the phone book to get ideas for guest speakers for my Tuesday luncheon Optimists' Club. A listing caught my attention: Suicide Helpline (24-hour) 458-7777. I dialed the number and was put in touch with the founder of the Denver operation. He agreed to speak before our group.
>
> His presentation touched me in two ways. First, the sheer number of calls astounded me (there were approximately ten-thousand per year when he spoke, and now the number exceeds twelve-thousand!). Second was the fact that this type of service epitomized true Christian giving from the heart, without expecting or receiving any reward. The telephone counselors remain anonymous to the callers and the callers themselves remain anonymous. Most often, the counselors never hear back from the people they help.
>
> I was interested in becoming a telephone counselor, but always had "more important things to do" than enroll in the lengthy training program. An incident nearly a year and a half

later finally moved me to action. In conjunction with my Optimists' Club, I was assigned the task of organizing an oratorical contest for junior and senior high-school boys and girls. The students were to prepare a five-minute speech on the topic "I think the best, I expect the best."

I managed to get a handful of local boys and girls to participate by visiting a number of area schools. When the night came for the contest, I was pleased beyond expectation. Every speech was moving and dealt with the students' personal backgrounds and how they used positive thinking to overcome obstacles in the path toward achievement. One young man spoke of his own triumphs against peer pressure and drug and alcohol abuse to become an outstanding student and athlete. I had looked forward to having him come back to our club as a featured luncheon speaker.

Several months later, I called his high-school guidance counselor for his home number. I'll never forget the call, when I learned that the young man had taken his own life after coming home from drinking with his friends. He had had words with his parents and then went into his room and shot himself.

A suicide leaves so many unanswered questions. . . . What caused him to backslide to drinking? What problem was so huge to a sixteen-year-old boy that he no longer wanted to live? Did he really comprehend what a final, irreversible step he was taking?

I knew I would never get the answers to those questions, but I had to address them at a level deeper than the Optimists' Creed. I had an opportunity within my grasp to avert a future tragedy, and I enrolled in the suicide prevention program. Every Tuesday night, now, I man the Lifeline.

AFTERWORD

New involvement in life is a process of border crossing. As we encounter unmet needs in the world, we are likely to come upon some significant limitations of our own. We become more productive—more of who we are—only as we acknowledge our limits, address them as directly as we can, and venture on. In employment, as in every sphere of life, we grow through our contingencies; the proving ground of vocation is at the boundary of our present lives. The deepest work involves us there.

I appreciate some of the commentaries on crossing borders in the Bible. They remind me of what it means and how it feels to move ahead as a human being. Many of the most vivid Biblical incidents have to do with water. The earliest Hebrews follow Moses through a sea in which their pursuers are thought to be drowned. Struggling through a dry and barren land, they come upon a formidable natural barrier: the River Jordan. The Jordan was not large, compared to the Mississippi or the Nile. At its widest, southern part near the Dead Sea, the Jordan is only ninety to a hundred feet wide, three to ten feet deep. It could be crossed.

But the River Jordan was perilous. "Jordan" is derived from the verb "to drop"; it falls about six hundred feet in the course of its eighty miles through Palestine, and the current is swift with whirlpools and rapids. Miss the ford, step off into a ten-foot depression, find yourself caught in the rapids, and you were in trouble. Especially if you were a desert nomad who had never seen a river this size before, who certainly couldn't swim!

The passage I find especially meaningful is Jesus' baptism in the Jordan by his cousin, John. It's an incident about which we know little. How did John perform baptism—a kind of cleansing rite, the origins of which are unclear? Students of the subject believe the Baptists have a point: he probably dunked people, submerged them for a moment in the River Jordan. Where in the river did he do this? We really have no idea. Wherever John performed his baptisms, though, and however he did it, we can be certain that for people of the desert the experience of submersion in a river was bound to be traumatic. Finding oneself under water, a nonswimmer in a swift-flowing river, was an experience likely to evoke fear. And also perhaps to recall the tribal memory of a nomadic people, crossing miles of barren land, only to encounter the first river most of them had ever seen.

I can imagine Jesus at the River Jordan with its rushing waters and the chill he might have felt treading the verge, back and forth along the bank, watching the disheveled John immersing people out there in the middle of the river. Perhaps that baptism experience called to mind the first Hebrew nomads who came upon the river, fought their anxiety through, and waded in.

There is an indefinite quality to the desert. Wandering there, one loses points of reference; after a time everything can look the same. If one facet of the landscape rises in prominence, the traveler can be deceived. Out on the desert one may fall victim to a mirage. But not before the river. The river stands, symbolically, at the boundary of life's next phase. The river is strange, foreign; it demarcates the new, uncharted land that lies ahead. And it reminds us, whatever our concerns, that in faith we can live fully on the next frontier.

APPENDIX

The following material includes a critical review of the principal types of employment service available today in the United States, some sources of overview on employment, and a list of resources for special interests.

RESOURCES FOR SEEKING PAID EMPLOYMENT

There is no shortage of agencies that purport to assist Americans who seek employment. Certain kinds of agencies are helpful in meeting specific needs, but it is important in approaching them to understand their specialized functions. Jeffrey Sonnenfeld's recent book, *Managing Career Systems: Channeling the Flow of Executive Careers*, offers a helpful review of the principal types of employment organizations: outplacement services, executive search firms, career counseling/career management services, and unemployment services. Sonnenfeld's comments are quoted below, followed by my own observations:

> *Outplacement* as a service grew out of the 1973–1975 economic slowdown when many companies were forced to pare management ranks. Recent increases in the number of mergers, acquisitions, plant closings, and worker displacement due to tech-

143

nology change or import substitution have also spurred the demand for mechanisms to handle dismissed employees. Today three-fourths of the nation's largest corporations as well as a number of governmental institutions provide either in-house outplacement or engage the services of an outside contractor . . . the fees of the outplacement firm are usually paid for by the former employer (usually 10 to 15 percent of the fired worker's annual salary, plus expenses).   (pp. 336–37)

Most outplacement services are oriented and restricted to upper management personnel. That is one limitation. The other is that they are intended to provide long-range career assistance at a time of job loss when most people find it difficult to plan. The experience of being fired is not a teachable moment!

The modern *executive search* industry grew out of recommendations made by general management consultants in the 1950's. As client companies were urged to reorganize, positions were created that couldn't always be filled internally. This required an outside search for talent, something that consultants naturally developed as an adjunct to their established business. Annual gross search billings during the 1950's were on the order of $500,000 for the entire industry. . . . During the 1970's there was a dramatic increase in the use of search firms. . . . During the last four years the search industry has grown by 74 percent. . . . Industry observers estimate that there are probably 1700 search firms of varying size doing business in the United States. . . . Traditionally, firms have generally charged about 30 percent of the starting salary to perform a search. Currently, the range seems to be between 20–60 percent.   (pp. 328–30)

Executive search firms are excellent sources of jobs similar to what one has. Prospective employers generally are unwilling to invest the amounts of money Sonnenfeld describes in novices or career changers. If one seeks a certain specialized position (such as retail-accounting management) for which he is qualified, executive search firms may be a good resource. The best firms specialize by industry. To find them, call some human-resource managers of companies in the desired industry and locale and ask which search firms they employ. Then make direct contact with the search firms.

> *Career counseling firms* charge large fees for their services . . . some firms charge 10 percent of the salary level desired. . . . Over the last few years, a lot of accusations have been made against career counseling firms. These complaints usually center around the fact that the firms do not provide the results they promise in their advertisements. (p. 335)

Two recent articles describe the inner workings of private career management firms that are objects of investigation and litigation in a number of states: Lee Guthrie's "Career Counselors: Will They Lead You Down the Primrose Path?" *Savvy* Magazine, December 1981; and Grant Pick's "The Executive Search," *TWA Ambassador*. I recommend reading them before enrolling in any private, packaged career counseling program.

Good career counselors charge no more for their services than do good psychotherapists. They have sufficient counseling skills to deal sensitively with the emotional stress that can accompany employment problems, but they do not confuse career counseling with psychotherapy and they refer clients with severe emotional problems to therapists. Career counselors also differ from psychotherapists in that they typically are more knowledgeable of their local labor market. They are able to assess not only the compatibility of job roles with clients, but also the availability of those jobs in a particular labor market.

There is at present no meaningful system of licensing career counselors. Good people in the field come from widely disparate academic and professional backgrounds, although most have some formal training in counseling and some business experience. Career counseling is a prime example of an emerging occupational role based on multidisciplinary skills, a la the information manager.

The best sources of referral to reputable career counselors are university placement offices, psychotherapists, and executive search consultants.

> *Government employment services* are state administered, but subject to federal control, since states receive financial support from federal tax rebates. . . . The services provided vary from state to state. The state employment agencies do not charge for their services. Unfortunately, many employers tend to think that well-qualified employees find work through other channels, so they look to the government employment services for less skilled labor. Thus, well-qualified people do not bother looking there, with the result that a vicious cycle begins. (p. 336)

Unemployment insurance in the United States at present is unrelated to any systematic, comprehensive retraining effort. It serves as a source of temporary income to those who lose their jobs, and little else. For a recent critique of the program, see Robert Reich's *The Next American Frontier.*

RESOURCES FOR UNDERSTANDING LABOR MARKET CHANGE

Several organizations offer occasional publications on broad issues affecting employment. These materials are not intended to help individuals seek work, but they offer insights into long-range trends affecting the labor market. Some of the best "overview" organizations are:

Worldwatch Institute
1776 Massachusetts Avenue NW
Washington, DC 20036
World Future Society
4916 St. Elmo Avenue
Bethesda, MD 10814-5089

National Occupational Information
   Coordinating Committee
   2100 M Street NW, Suite 156
   Washington, DC 20037

American Society for Training and Development
   600 Maryland Avenue SW, Suite 305
   Washington, DC 20024

National Institute for Work and Learning
   1200 18th Street NW, Suite 316
   Washington, DC 20036

RESOURCES FOR SPECIAL INTERESTS AND CONCERNS

New Ways to Work is a San Francisco-based organization that supports new work formats such as job sharing and flextime. Their address is: 149 Ninth Street, San Francisco, CA 94130. Phone: (415) 552-1000.

Warren Ziegler's Futures-Invention Associates sponsor workshops for organizations and communities wishing to imagine and plan alternative futures. Their address is: 2260 Fairfax Street, Denver, CO 80207. Phone: (303) 399-1077.

The headquarters of the Johnson O'Connor Foundation, which offers aptitude testing in a dozen offices throughout the country, is: 11 East 62nd Street, New York, NY 10021. Phone: (212) 838-0550.

Volunteer! A Comprehensive Guide to Voluntary Service in the United States and Abroad, published by the Council on International Education Exchange: Commission on Voluntary Service and Action, offers information on service opportunities. It is available for $5.50 from Intercultural Press, PO Box 768, Yarmouth, ME 04096. The Voluntary Service Bulletin is published annually by the Presbyterian

Church of the USA, 475 Riverside Drive, Room 1126, New York, NY 10115.

The best source of information on local volunteer opportunities such as Lifeline is the United Way.

Several innovative organizations offer assistance in small business development. Control Data Corporation has sponsored a number of Business and Technology Centers to provide comprehensive, computer-assisted support for business development, with an emphasis on economic revitalization of depressed areas. Information can be obtained from Business and Technology Centers Development Program, Control Data Corporation, Box P, Minneapolis, MN 55440. Phone: (612) 853-5658.

The federal Small Business Administration serves as a clearinghouse for information on a number of similar, small business "incubator/greenhouses" providing comprehensive start-up services for those who wish to build a business from a promising idea. The agency to contact is: Office of Private Sector Initiatives, Small Business Administration, 1441 L Street NW, Washington, DC 20036.

Partnership for Productivity is a similar business development program for enterprises in the Third World. Originally funded through the Friends World Committee for Consultation's Right Sharing of World Resources Program, PFP now is established as an independent, not-for-profit agency in developing nations of Africa, Latin America, and the Caribbean. For further information, contact Partnership for Productivity International, 2001 S Street NW, Suite 610, Washington, DC 20009. Phone: (202) 483-0067.

The Overseas List (see Bibliography) is a recent, comprehensive book on opportunities for service in developing countries.

Peacework Alternatives is a national organization that "encourages discussion of the ethical aspects of defense work, seeks to provide a network of services for defense workers in struggle, and works toward economic conversion." Its address is: 3940 Poplar Level Road, Louisville, KY 40213.

High Technology Professionals for Peace is a similar organization, oriented to engineers and scientists, at: 639 Massachusetts Avenue, Room 316, Cambridge, MA 02139. Phone: (617) 497-0605.

Information on defense involvement and investment practices of US corporations can be obtained from the Interfaith Center on Corporate Responsibility, National Council of Churches, 475 Riverside Drive, Room 566, New York, NY 10115. Phone: (212) 870-2936.

The Academy of Independent Scholars is an association of "retirement age" scholars who wish to continue their creative activities through publication and mentorship. The address is: PO Box 3247, Boulder, CO 80307.

The Center for Professional Ethics at Manhattan College provides conferences, workshops, and professional training programs on ethical concerns in diverse fields such as business, engineering, education, and nursing. It serves as a resource center for professionals in these areas and publishes a biannual newsletter. For further information contact: Dr. John Wilcox, Director, Center for Professional Ethics, Manhattan College, Riverdale, NY 10471. Phone: (212) 920-0114.

The Foresight System, which I have developed from David Kolb's research, is an alternative to outplacement programs, based on proactive planning. Further information on the Foresight System and the Professional Career Development Program (a cost-efficient, computer-supported program of employment services for individuals) is available from me at the University of Denver, Denver, CO 80208.

BIBLIOGRAPHY

Beckmann, David M. et al. *The Overseas List: Opportunities for Living and Working in Developing Countries.* Minneapolis: Augsburg, 1985.

Berg, Ivar. *Education and Jobs: The Great Training Robbery.* New York: Praeger, 1970.

Blakney, R. B., trans. Lao Tsu, *The Way of Life/Tao Te Ching.* New York: New American Library of World Literature, Mentor Books, 1955.

Boorstin, Daniel. *The Discoverers: A History of Man's Search to Know His World and Himself.* New York: Vintage, 1983.

Buber, Martin. *Between Man and Man.* New York: Macmillan, 1965.

Charland, William A. Jr. "Career Roles." *Western's World, The Magazine of Western Airlines,* November/December 1981.

———. "Contracts and Covenants: A Model for Interracial Social Action." *Pastoral Psychology,* May 1970.

———. *Decide to Live: Adult Approaches to Values.* Philadelphia: Westminster, 1979.

Chickering, Arthur W. and Associates. *The Modern American College.* San Francisco: Jossey-Bass, 1981.

Crichton, Michael. *Five Patients: The Hospital Explained.* New York: Knopf, 1970.

Cornish, Edward. "The Coming of an Information Society." *The Futurist,* April 1981.

Crowell, George. *Society against Itself.* Philadelphia: Westminster, 1968.

Doctorow, E. L. *Loon Lake.* New York: Random House, 1980.

Erikson, Erik. *Identity: Youth and Crisis.* New York: Norton, 1968.

Evans, Christopher. *The Micro Millennium.* New York: Washington Square Press, 1981.

Fallows, James. "The Case against Credentialism." *The Atlantic Monthly,* December 1985.

Farb, Peter. *Man's Rise to Civilization: As Shown by the Indians of North America from Primeval Times to the Coming of the Industrial State.* New York: Discus/Avon, 1968.

Ferre, Nels F. S. *The Finality of Faith and Christianity among the World Religions.* New York: Harper & Row, 1963.

Fowles, John. *Daniel Martin.* Boston: Little, Brown, 1977.

Friedman, Milton and Rose. *Free to Choose: A Personal Statement.* New York: Avon, 1981.

Fromm, Erich. *Man for Himself.* New York: Holt, Rinehart and Winston, 1947.

Galbraith, John Kenneth. *The New Industrial State.* Boston: Houghton Mifflin, 1968.

Gardner, John. *The Art of Living and Other Stories.* New York: Knopf, 1981.

Garreau, Joel. *The Nine Nations of North America.* New York: Avon, 1981.

Germann, Richard. *Job and Career Building.* Berkeley: Ten Speed Press, 1980.

Gilligan, Carol. *In a Different Voice: Psychological Theory and Women's Development.* Cambridge: Harvard University Press, 1982.

The Global 2000 Report to the President: Entering the Twenty-First Century. Washington, DC: US Government Printing Office, 1980.

Gould, Roger. *Transformations.* New York: Simon and Schuster, 1978.

Harmon, Willis. "Chronic Unemployment: An Emerging Problem of Postindustrial Society" in *Careers Tomorrow* edited by Edward Cornish. Bethesda, Maryland: World Future Society, 1983.

Jacobs, Jane. *Cities and the Wealth of Nations: Principles of Economic Life.* New York: Random House, 1984.

Jorgenson, James. *The Graying of America: Retirement and Why You Can't Afford It.* New York: McGraw Hill, 1981.

Jung, Carl. "Two Essays in Analytical Psychology" quoted in Fordham, Frieda. *An Introduction to Jung's Psychology.* New York: Pelican, 1953.

Kidron, Michael, and Segal, Ronald. *The New State of the World Atlas.* New York: Simon and Schuster, 1984.

Kierkegaard, Søren. *The Sickness Unto Death.* Translated by Walter Lowrie. Princeton: Princeton University Press, 1941.

Koehn, Hank. *Help Wanted 1990: Skills and Professions in the Decade Ahead.* Memphis: Center for the Study of Higher Education, Memphis State University, 1985.

Kolb, David A. *Experiential Learning: Experience as the Source of Learning and Development.* Englewood Cliffs, New Jersey: Prentice-Hall, 1984.

Kolbus, David. *SRI Business Intelligence Program.* Stanford, California: Stanford Research Institute, 1980.

Kouri, Mary. "The New Elders." Ph.D. dissertation, The Union Graduate School, 1982.

_____. *Elderlife: A Time to Give, A Time to Receive.* Denver: Human Growth and Development Associates, 1985.

Lamb, David. *The Africans.* New York: Vintage Books, 1984.

Lamm, Richard D. *Megatraumas: America in the Year 2000*. Boston: Houghton Mifflin, 1985.

Levinson, Daniel. *The Seasons of a Man's Life*. New York: Knopf, 1978.

McLeish, John. *The Ulyssean Adult: Creativity in the Middle and Later Years*. New York: McGraw-Hill Ryerson, 1976.

Masten, Ric and Billie Barbara. *His & Hers: a passage through the middle-age crazies*. Carmel, California: Sunflower Ink, 1978.

May, Rollo. *The Meaning of Anxiety*. New York: Ronald Press, 1950.

Naipaul, V. S. *Guerrillas*. New York: Random House, 1975.

———. *A Bend in the River*. New York: Random House, 1980.

Naisbitt, John. *Megatrends: Ten New Directions Transforming Our Lives*. New York: Warner Books, 1982.

——— and Aburdene, Patricia. *Re-Inventing the Corporation*. New York: Warner Books, 1985.

Norman, Colin. *Microelectronics at Work: Productivity and Jobs in the World Economy*. Washington, DC: Worldwatch Institute, 1980.

Reich, Robert. *The Next American Frontier*. New York: Penguin Books, 1983.

Rohrlich, Jay B. *Work and Love: The Crucial Balance*. New York: Crown, 1982.

Schumacher, E. F. *Small Is Beautiful: Economics as if People Mattered*. New York: Harper & Row, 1973.

——— and Gillingham, Peter. *Good Work*. New York: Harper Colophon Books, 1979.

Sonnenfeld, Jeffrey. *Managing Career Systems: Channeling the Flow of Executive Careers*. Homewood, Illinois: Irwin, 1984.

Suzuki, D. T. *The Field of Zen*. New York: Harper & Row, 1970.

Tawney, R. H. *Religion and the Rise of Capitalism: A Historical Study*. New York: Harcourt Brace, 1926.

Terkel, Studs. *Working: People Talk about What They Do All Day and How They Feel about What They Do*. New York: Random House, 1972.

Toffler, Alvin. *The Third Wave*. New York: Bantam Books, 1980.

———. *Future Shock*. New York: Random House, 1970.

Weber, Max. *The Protestant Ethic and the Spirit of Capitalism*. London: G. Allen and Unwin, 1952.

Willens, Harold. *The Trimtab Factor: How Business Executives Can Help Solve the Nuclear Weapons Crisis*. New York: Morrow, 1984.

Yankelovich, Daniel. *New Rules: Searching for Self-Fulfillment in a World Turned Upside Down*. New York: Random House, 1981.

COPYRIGHT ACKNOWLEDGMENTS